MASTERING THE FASB CODIFICATION AND eIFRS:
A CASE APPROACH

NATALIE T. CHURYK
Northern Illinois University

THOMAS C. PEARSON
University of Hawaii

THOMAS R. WEIRICH
Central Michigan University

WILEY

John Wiley & Sons, Inc.

VP & PUBLISHER:	George Hoffman
ACQUISITIONS EDITOR:	Michael Mcdonald
PROJECT EDITOR:	Brian Kamins
EDITORIAL ASSISTANT:	Jacqueline Kepping
SENIOR MARKETING MANAGER:	Karolina Zarychta
DESIGNER:	Seng Ping Ngieng
SENIOR PRODUCTION MANAGER:	Janis Soo
SENIOR PRODUCTION EDITOR:	Joyce Poh

Cover image © Courtney Keating/iStockphoto.

Permission granted from the AICPA to utilize topics from their AICPA Technical Practice Aids.

Images from the FASB Accounting Standards Codification TM are reproduced with permission from the Financial Accounting Foundation.

e-IFRS screenshots are reproduced with permission from the International Accounting Standards Board.

LexisNexis screenshots are reproduced with permission from LexisNexis, a division of Reed Elselvier Inc

RIA Checkpoint, published online at *http://checkpoint.riag.com* by Thomson Reuters/IRA C2011 reprinted with permission All rights reserved. This information or any portion of it may not be copied or disseminated in any form or by any means or stored in an electronic database or retrieval system without the express written consent of Thomson Reuter/RIA

This book was set in 10.5/12 Bodoni Standard by Thomson Digital and printed and bound by RR Donnelley. The cover was printed by RR Donnelley.

This book is printed on acid free paper.

Founded in 1807, John Wiley & Sons, Inc. has been a valued source of knowledge and understanding for more than 200 years, helping people around the world meet their needs and fulfill their aspirations. Our company is built on a foundation of principles that include responsibility to the communities we serve and where we live and work. In 2008, we launched a Corporate Citizenship Initiative, a global effort to address the environmental, social, economic, and ethical challenges we face in our business. Among the issues we are addressing are carbon impact, paper specifications and procurement, ethical conduct within our business and among our vendors, and community and charitable support. For more information, please visit our website: www.wiley.com/go/citizenship.

Evaluation copies are provided to qualified academics and professionals for review purposes only, for use in their courses during the next academic year. These copies are licensed and may not be sold or transferred to a third party. Upon completion of the review period, please return the evaluation copy to Wiley. Return instructions and a free of charge return shipping label are available at **www.wiley.com/go/returnlabel**. Outside of the United States, please contact your local representative.

Library of Congress Cataloging-in-Publication Data

Churyk, Natalie T.
   Mastering the FASB codification and eIFRS/Natalie T. Churyk, Thomas C. Pearson, Thomas R. Weirich.
     p. cm.
   Includes index.
   ISBN 978-1-118-10729-4 (pbk.)
1. Accounting–Standards–Databases. 2. Accounting–Research–Databases. I. Weirich, Thomas R. II. Pearson, Thomas C
III. Title.
   HF5626.C49 2012
   657.02'18–dc23

                        2011025461

Printed in the United States of America
10 9 8 7 6 5 4 3 2 1

CONTENTS

PREFACE

Welcome to the world of electronic financial accounting research. In today's environment, professional accountants that conduct financial accounting research will be utilizing some type of electronic research database. This text's objective is to provide you with the tools to conduct such research. It is intended for financial accounting classes, both undergraduate and graduate. It may be easily used as a supplementary text in intermediate or advanced accounting classes. This book is designed to serve both as a reference tool for the practitioner/student who desires to become proficient in conducting electronic financial accounting research and as a tool in honing one's research skills. Screen shots of various databases are incorporated in the text. Chapters 1–3 will provide you with the mechanics of maneuvering through the primary financial accounting databases.

Chapter 1 explains how to research U.S. generally accepted accounting principles (GAAP), which is now located in the Financial Accounting Standards Board (FASB) Accounting Standards Codification (ASC or the Codification). Given that the U.S. economy is a significant part of the global economy, even foreign students should learn how to research U.S. GAAP.

In the process of creating the ASC, U.S. GAAP is now shorter, more principled, and easier to research than the superseded U.S. GAAP. Since finding appropriate authority is easier than before the ASC, it more likely that more individuals will scrutinize financial accounting research in the future. Thus, accountants must take greater care to accurately research U.S. GAAP.

Chapter 2 explains how to research international financial reporting standards and other authorities associated with the International Accounting Standards Board (IASB). Even U.S. students need to understand the hierarchy of international accounting authorities and how to use the eIFRS electronic database to access the International Financial Reporting Standards (IFRS).

In 2007, the IASB was recognized by the U.S. Securities and Exchange Commission (SEC) as an official standard-setter in accounting. Foreign companies may now file their financial statements with the SEC using IASB's IFRS without reconciling to U.S. GAAP. It is possible that starting in 2015, U.S. public companies will start using IFRS if a comprehensive IFRS "work plan" to permit U.S. public companies to use IFRS is accepted by the SEC.

Chapter 3 presents an accounting database from RIA; the SEC's EDGAR database, where companies file financial reports: and two other major financial accounting research databases. These databases provide helpful information such as compiled financial ratios, insightful secondary sources, easier ability to compare companies, and sometimes analyst reports on a company. Some of the real-life cases in this text will show how companies monitor performance using financial ratios.

Chapter 4 presents short cases, which provide opportunities to practice basic skills in researching in the FASB's Codification, IASB's eIFRS, and other databases. We call these short cases Knowledge Busters. Mastery of these short cases helps novice researchers develop the skills to tackle the more in-depth hypothetical cases and real-life cases presented in the last chapter.

Chapter 5 presents cases that vary in length and depth of analysis. Part A consists of hypothetical cases on important recent issues faced in the accounting profession. Part B presents six real-life cases, simplified for an easier understanding of the challenges faced by the companies. Given that public companies are used, students must also consider the SEC part of the Codification for U.S. GAAP. Often students must compare U.S. GAAP standards to the relevant international standards. Besides researching the issues, students must consider strategic elements in these cases. The questions at the end of each case are designed to help students think critically through the case. Some cases invite role-playing in class as a means of discussing the cases. The authors' website provides assistance in using the text for various classes.

Gratitude is extended to the authors' former students and professional colleagues for providing insights as to the research needs of future Certified Public Accountants. A specific thank-you is extended to all those granting permission to utilize their databases, the technical support provided by the staff of Wiley, and the encouragement provided by our families for writing this essential textbook.

Natalie T. Churyk
Northern Illinois University

Thomas C. Pearson
University of Hawaii

Thomas R. Weirich
Central Michigan University

ABOUT THE AUTHORS

Natalie Tatiana Churyk, Ph.D., is the Caterpillar Professor of Accountancy at Northern Illinois University. She earned her Doctorate in Accounting with a Finance Cognate from the University of South Carolina. She received her B.S. in Accounting and her M.B.A. with a specialization in Finance from California State University, Long Beach. Dr. Churyk has public accounting experience with a local California firm.

Dr. Churyk has coauthored *Accounting and Auditing Research: Tools and Strategies* and is the FAR contributor for *Wiley CPA Exam Review 2012* and *Wiley CPA Exam Review 39*th*Edition*. She has published in professional journals such as the *Journal of Accountancy, Strategic Finance,* and the *CPA Journal*. She also has various publications in academic journals such as the *Journal of Business Research* and *Journal of Accounting Education*. Dr. Churyk has received research grants from PricewaterhouseCoopers, the Institute of Management Accountants, and her university.

Dr. Churyk teaches in the undergraduate and M.A.S. programs. Additionally, she develops and delivers continuing professional education in Northern Illinois University's CPA and CIA Review programs. Service has included holding officer positions in and chairing several of the American Accounting Association's Teaching, Learning and Curriculum section and Forensic and Investigative Accounting section committees. She has also served on various national and state committees related to education, student, or women's initiatives.

Thomas C. Pearson, LL.M., J.D., CPA, is a Professor of Accounting at the University of Hawaii at Manoa and former Director of its School of Accountancy. He earned two Masters of Letters of Law in tax from New York University and the University of Denver, a Doctorate of Jurisprudence and an M.B.A. from Vanderbilt University, and an A.B. from Dartmouth College. Professor Pearson received the George A. Katz Memorial Award in Securities Law in 2005. He has previously taught at the University of Wyoming and National Taiwan University. He has previous work experience at Hospital Corporation of America.

Professor Pearson has published about 40 articles, including articles in the *Stanford Journal of Law, Business and Finance, North Carolina Journal of International Law and Commercial Regulation,* and *Review of Banking and Financial Law*. He has also published in leading academic accounting journals such as *Accounting Horizons, Journal of Accounting Education,* and *Journal of the American Taxation Association*.

Numerous teaching awards include the University of Hawaii's Board of Regents Teaching Excellence Award and the Outstanding Achievement in Education Award of the Hawaii Society of CPAs. He has served as President of the Shidler College of Business Faculty Senate and on numerous university committees. He has also served on Hawaii's Tax Review Commission and is involved in several professional organizations.

Thomas R. Weirich, Ph.D., CPA, is currently the Jerry and Felicia Campbell Endowed Professor of Accounting at Central Michigan University and former Chair of its School of Accounting. He earned a Doctorate in Accountancy from the University of Missouri–Columbia, as well as M.B.A. and B.S. degrees from Northern Illinois University. Dr. Weirich has public accounting experience with both an international firm and a local firm. He has served as the Academic Fellow to the Office of Chief Accountant at the

U.S. Securities and Exchange Commission and has held a Faculty in Residence position with Arthur Andersen, LLP, in its Business Fraud and Investigative Services Division. Dr. Weirich has also served as a consultant to the Public Oversight Board's Panel on Audit Effectiveness and as an expert witness for the SEC and several other organizations.

Dr. Weirich has written numerous articles in professional journals and has assisted others by, for example, serving on the Editorial Advisory Board to the *Journal of Accountancy.* Dr. Weirich has received many teaching and professional awards, including the School of Accounting/Beta Alpha Psi's Outstanding Teaching Award, Ameritech/SBC Teaching Award, College of Business Dean's Teaching Award, Michigan Association of Governing Boards' Distinguished Faculty Award, and Michigan Association of CPAs' Distinguished Achievement in Accounting Education Award.

Extensive service was performed for national, state, and local committees, such as the American Accounting Association's Education Committee, the SEC Liaison Committee, the American Institute of Certified Professional Accountants' SEC Regulations Committee, and the Board of Examiners' Auditing Subcommittee that aids in the development of the Certified Professional Accountant examination. Dr. Weirich has also served as mayor of Mt. Pleasant, Michigan, and has spent many years on its City Commission. He currently serves as Chair of the Michigan's Board of Accountancy.

FASB Accounting Standards Codification^{TM} Research System

T he Financial Accounting Standards Board (FASB) Codification^{TM} Research System (the Codification) enables comprehensive, but not complete, research on accounting issues for the private sector. The Codification includes essential[1] content and implementation guidance from prior generally accepted accounting principles (GAAP) levels A–D and organizes this information into approximately ninety topical areas, described later in this chapter. A master glossary is also contained in the Codification.

To provide users with a more comprehensive database, the Codification team included limited Securities and Exchange Commission (SEC) content (Regulation S-X, Financial Reporting Releases, Accounting Series Releases, Interpretive Releases, Staff Accounting Bulletins, EITF Topic D, and SEC Staff Observer Comments) in the Codification. SEC content in the Codification is labeled with the letter "S." The included SEC literature is for user convenience only, and the researcher should be aware that SEC sources follow a traditional legal hierarchy.

Upon adoption, the Codification superseded all preexisting nongovernmental accounting and reporting standards. The Codification replaced the prior five-level GAAP[2] hierarchy with two levels: authoritative and nonauthoritative. Thus, the Codification supersedes the following standards and implementation guidance issued by the FASB and prior standard-setters:

1. The FASB category contains Statement of Financial Accounting Standards (SFAS); Interpretations (FIN), which clarify, explain, or elaborate on prior FASB, Accounting Principles Board (APB), and Accounting Research Bulletin (ARB) statements; Technical Bulletins (FTB), which provide guidance in applying pronouncements; Staff Positions (FSP); Implementation Guides (Q&A); and SFAS No. 138 examples, "Accounting for Certain Derivative Instruments and Certain Hedging Activities."

2. The Emerging Issues Task Force (EITF) category includes Abstracts that are the result of research related to new and unusual financial transactions or controversial issues. The EITF reaches a consensus on how to account for the specific transaction and then releases an Abstract. Topic D includes other technical matters related to the implications and implementations of the Abstracts.

3. The Derivatives Implementation Group (DIG) was organized in 1998 and had its last meeting in 2001. Its primary purpose was to examine issues related to derivatives and hedges. Among its 189 issuances, some were previously superseded, some were integrated into SFAS No. 133, and some were revised to meet current market conditions.

---

[1] While developing the Codification Research System, the Codification team organized literature into essential and nonessential literature. Essential content includes items such as implementation guidance and the actual standard. Only essential content is codified. Nonessential content includes items such as the basis for FASB dissension, summaries, background information, and similar content. Nonessential content is located in an archived standard and available by means of the left navigation panel of the Codification.

[2] FASB, SFAS No. 162, "The Hierarchy of Generally Accepted Accounting Principles" (2008).

4. Thirty-one opinions of the American Institute of Certified Public Accountants (AICPA) APB, along with Accounting Interpretations (AIN), were still in effect in 2009. (Many were previously superseded.)

5. Fifty-one ARBs were issued by the Committee on Accounting Procedures (CAP) of the AICPA.

6. The AICPA category contains Statements of Position (SOP); Audit and Accounting Guides (AAG) (only incremental accounting guidance that normally is reviewed by the AICPA Accounting Standards Executive Committee, or AcSEC, and cleared by the FASB); Practice Bulletins (PB) (including the Notices to Practitioners elevated to Practice Bulletin status by Practice Bulletin 1); and Technical Inquiry Services (TIS) for Software Revenue Recognition only.

CODIFICATION ACCESS

Access the Codification from the FASB website (www.fasb.org), as shown in Figure 1.1, or go directly to www.asc.fasb.org, as shown in Figure 1.2. There are two types of users and two subscriptions available:

1. Login—Left-clicking on this box will provide login access for non-academic users. First time users must order the basic or professional view, described below.

    a. Basic View—The basic view is free to users that register with a valid email address. It has limited functionality. Users can browse by topic, locate legacy (archived) standards, and utilize basic print functions.

    b. Professional View—The professional view provides full access to the Codification for a fee. Users can browse by topic, keyword search, advanced search, or glossary. Additionally, users can go directly to a code section, join content, cross-reference from archived standards, print with or without references, and access archived/legacy standards. Each of these functions is discussed later in the chapter.

2. Academic—The academic subscription provides faculty and students access to the professional view of the Codification at a reduced rate through the American Accounting Association. Users that subscribe will left-click this area to access the Codification, as shown in Figure 1.3.

FIGURE 1.1 CODIFICATION LOCATION

FIGURE 1.2 | REGISTRATION OPTIONS

 ACCOUNTING STANDARDS CODIFICATION®

Professional View

Annual Subscription $850 - Discounts for Multiple Users
Concurrent use product, providing full functionality and advanced navigation including:

- **Browsing** by Topic, **Searching**, and **Go To** navigation
- **Joining and Combining Content** feature for viewing user-selected excerpts
- **Cross Reference** report and archive to locate and access legacy standards
- Various **Printing** options, including *printer-friendly* utility for viewing source references
- **Archive** feature for accessing any previous version of the content
- **Glossary** term display feature for quickly viewing definitions
- **What's New** feature for accessing recently issued content
- **What Links Here** feature for identifying content related to a specific paragraph
- **Email** feature for sending comments to colleagues
- Personal **Annotations** feature for keeping notes about selected content
- **Copy and Paste** functionality
- Current **Location & Heading Depth** feature for quickly assessing where you are.

Academic View

Free access to Professional View

- Accounting program faculty and students go to *Academic Accounting Access*

Basic View

Free access:

- Browsing by Topic
- Limited print functionality
- Utility to identify the location of legacy standards.

- **Login**

- **Order Professional or Basic View**

- **Academic Accounting Access**
  (Academic Accounting Faculty and Students)

View the 45-page description of the structure and content of the FASB Codification.

Notice to Constituents—About the Codification 📄

FIGURE 1.3 | ACADEMIC USER ACCESS

Academic Accounting Access
An initiative of the American Accounting Association and Financial Accounting Foundation

FASB Accounting Standards Codification™
Professional View

**Financial Accounting Foundation
and American Accounting Association
to Provide FASB Codification to Accounting Faculty and Students**

Registered User Login | Enrollment Form | Renewal Form

Frequently Asked Questions

FIGURE 1.4   CODIFICATION OPENING SCREEN

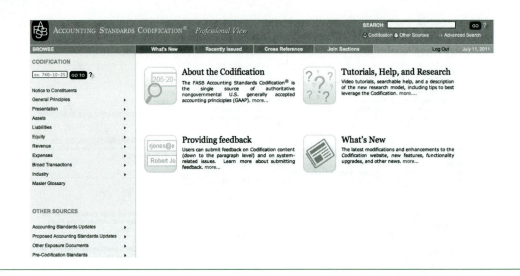

THE CODIFICATION

The Codification opening screen appears in Figure 1.4. There are five tabs: Browse, What's New, Recently Issued, Cross Reference, and Join Sections. Four of the five tabs, described below, are located along the top of the center screen area. The What's New tab includes information by date, topic, or document for various time periods, up to one year. The Recently Issued tab includes links to recently issued content. The Cross Reference tab allows the researcher to cross-reference between the original archived standards and the Codification. This is very useful for researchers familiar with prior GAAP levels. For instance, as demonstrated in Figure 1.5, the researcher can select a type of standard (APB, EITF, FIN, etc.) from the Standard Type drop-down menu. The Standard Number drop-down menu is populated based on the standard type selected. The researcher then left-clicks the Generate Report button to produce a report cross-referencing each standard paragraph to the Codification. The Join Sections tab allows the researcher to select multiple topics and display those choices in one document. For instance, the researcher can select a topic and section utilizing a drop-down menu, as displayed in Figure 1.6. The researcher can choose to include or exclude intersection subtopics and choose among FASB, SEC, and all material. By left-clicking the Get Sections button, a report is generated, as shown in the bottom half of part A of Figure 1.6. The researcher then selects the desired sections and left-clicks the Join Sections button, and a report similar to part B in Figure 1.6 is generated. The researcher has the option to expand or collapse the joined material once the report is generated.

The Browse tab is a powerful research tool and is further divided into three areas: the left navigation panel, which provides access to the Codification and other sources; the center screen area, which provides access to items such as tutorials and providing feedback, and the top right screen area, which provides a Search bar. Each item appearing on the Browse tab is briefly discussed below, from left to right and top to bottom. Some items are discussed in detail later in the chapter when covering topics such as research.

FIGURE 1.5 | CROSS REFERENCE OPTION

Cross Reference

Use this feature to cross reference between the original standards and the Codification. Insert information about a standard to identify the Codification Sections that contain the content. Alternatively, insert information about the Codification to identify the standards that populated that portion of the Codification. Click here for help with or to view a tutorial on the Cross Reference feature. NOTE: The report only includes content contained in published Topics. Click here to view the details of the standard type acronyms.

By Standard ?

Standard Type	Standard Number
FAS ▾	123(R) ▾

or

By Codification ?

Topic	Subtopic	Section	Paragraph
-	-	-	

GENERATE REPORT   START OVER

Sort your results by *Standard Type* or by *Topic*.

PAGES: 1 | 2 ▶

▼Standard Type	Standard Number	Paragraph / Label	Sequence	Topic	Subtopic	Section	Paragraph
FAS	123(R)	1	76.1.1	718	10	10	10-2
FAS	123(R)	1	76.1.2	718	10	30	30-4
FAS	123(R)	1	76.2.1	505	50	10	10-1
FAS	123(R)	1	76.2.2	718	10	10	10-1
FAS	123(R)	1	76.2.2	505	50	05	05-9
FAS	123(R)	4	80.1	718	10	15	15-7

FIGURE 1.6 | JOIN SECTIONS OPTION

(A) Join Sections Input and Preliminary Output for Selection

Join Sections

The Join Sections function allows you to select Codification content that spans multiple Topics and Subtopics. You must select a Topic AND a Section. Click here for help with or to view a tutorial on the Join Sections feature.

Options

Topic	605 - Revenue Recognition ▾ ?	Exclude Intersection Subtopics ▾ ?
Section	05 - Overview and Background ▾ ?	FASB only ▾ ?

GET SECTIONS

JOIN SECTIONS

Sort your results by *Standard Type* or by *Topic*.

☐	Topic	Subtopic	Section	Title
☐	605	10	05	605 Revenue Recognition > 10 Overall > 05 Background
☐	605	15	05	605 Revenue Recognition > 15 Products > 05 Background
☐	605	20	05	605 Revenue Recognition > 20 Services > 05 Background
☐	605	25	05	605 Revenue Recognition > 25 Multiple-Element Arrangements > 05 Background
☐	605	28	05	605 Revenue Recognition > 28 Milestone Method > 05 Background

(B) Join Sections Result

Table of Contents
Collapse | Expand

⊟ 605 Revenue Recognition
　⊞ 15 Products
　⊞ 25 Multiple-Element Arrangements

Browse Tab—Left Navigation Panel

The left navigation panel is divided into two areas: Codification and Other Sources. This panel remains on the screen regardless of which tab or which heading the researcher clicks on. Each heading in the left navigation panel is discussed below. Search strategies utilizing topical categories and the master glossary are discussed later in the chapter.

Codification

1. Go To box—If the researcher is familiar with a desired code section, the researcher can type the code section in the box and be hyperlinked to that particular section.

2. Notice to Constituents—The Notice to Constituents is a forty-five-page document describing the Codification in detail. It discusses the Codification in general, its goals, its content, its functionality, its structure, future standard setting, and background material.

3. Topical Categories—The topical categories (described below) include General Principles, Presentation, financial statement accounts (Assets, Liabilities, Equity, Revenue, Expenses), Broad Transactions, and Industry.

   a. General Principle topics are assigned codes 105–199 and cover conceptual matters such as GAAP. As of July 2011, most of the content was still pending.

   b. Presentation topics are assigned codes 205–299 and include, for example, Comprehensive Income (220), Notes to the Financial Statements (235), and Segment Reporting (280).

   c. Financial statement accounts topics are numbered from 305–799 and appear separately in the left navigation panel: Assets (305–399), Liabilities (405–499), Equity (505–599), Revenue (605–699), and Expenses (705–799). Examples of topics within the financial statement accounts include Inventory (330), Contingencies (450), and Research and Development (730).

   d. Broad Transactions topics are assigned codes between 805 and 899. Because some topics, such as Business Combinations (805) and Interest (835), affect more than one financial statement, they are considered to be transactions-oriented and are included in this area.

   e. Industry topics are assigned codes 905–999 and include unique accounting topics such as Development Stage Enterprises (915).

      The topical categories follow a three-two-two numbering scheme (XXX-YY-ZZ). Topics are assigned three-digit codes between 105 and 999, as described above. Subtopics are subsets (type or scope) of the topics. For example, 15 Products and 20 Services are subtopics of Revenue (605). The subtopics are further refined into sections from 00 to 99. For consistency, section numbers do not change. For instance, section 05 refers to Overview and Background and section 20 refers to the Glossary whether the researcher is examining the Business Combinations subtopic of Overall (10) or Reverse Acquisitions (40). Subsections refine sections in a limited number of cases. Figure 1.7[3] provides a visual representation of the numbering schematic used by the Codification. When citing the Codification, the researcher will preface the code numbers with ASC (Accounting Standards Codification). For instance, the citation for Capital Leases Disclosure for Lessees is ASC 840-30-50-1.

4. Master Glossary—The master glossary provides a list of all glossary terms contained in each topic.

---

[3] Modified from the Codification Notice to Constituents, www.asc.fasb.org/ (2008).

FIGURE 1.7 | CODIFICATION CODING STRUCTURE

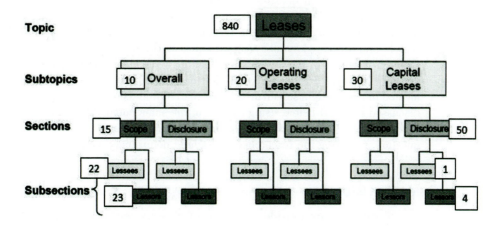

Source: Modified from the Notice to Constituents in the Codification.

Other Sources Other Sources includes five items: Accounting Standards Updates, Proposed Accounting Standards Updates, Other Exposure Documents, Pre-Codification Standards, and Maintenance Updates. Pre-Codification Standards link the researcher to FASB and AICPA standards. Researchers more familiar with superseded authoritative literature will find this link useful for input into the cross-reference function described earlier. Maintenance Updates are editorial corrections to the Codification.

Browse Tab—Center Screen Area

The center screen area contains the following headings: About the Codification; Providing feedback; Tutorial, Help, and Research, and What's New. What's New was described earlier. The remaining areas are discussed below.

1. About the Codification—links to the Notice to Constituents. The Notice to Constituents can also be found near the top of the left navigation panel, as described earlier.

2. Providing feedback—links to information about how to provide content feedback and overall system-related feedback.

3. Tutorials, help and research—provides audio slide deck tutorials, help on navigation (browsing, searching, and go to), help on other features such as annotations, archived content, copy and paste, feedback, glossaries, joining content, location, pending content, printing, SEC content, and XBRL and four suggestions for researching in the Codification.

Browse Tab—Top Right Screen Area

The top right screen area contains a Search box and a link to the Advanced Search. Both search features are discussed in detail in the following pages.

THE RESEARCH PROCESS

The Codification database enables researchers to obtain authoritative evidence to help answer their research questions more efficiently than they could using manual hard-bound tools. In addition to the cross-reference search discussed above, search processes in the Codification include using the master glossary, performing a topical category search, and utilizing keyword search inquiries. The location of each search process is shown in Figure 1.4, the Codification opening screen. The master glossary and topical categories options are located in the left navigation panel, and the search function is located in the top right screen area. Each search process (except for advanced search) is discussed in detail below, using aspects of the same company to validate the research method. Note that the Codification may not contain guidance for the researcher's question, requiring the researcher to examine nonprimary support.

Master Glossary

The master glossary provides a list of all glossary terms contained in each topical category. To use the master glossary, left-click on the Master Glossary heading. As illustrated in Figure 1.8, the alphabet will appear in the center screen area along with a Glossary Term Quick Find option. Left-click the desired letter or type in a term. If a letter is clicked, scroll down to the area of interest and left-click on the term to display its definition. If a term is entered in the Quick Find area, all glossary terms containing the term of interest will be displayed in the center screen area. For example, if the term "lease" is entered in the Quick Find area, the terms "lease," "lease term," and "capital lease" will appear in the center screen area. Left-click the desired term to display the definition. Once in the definition, left-click on the Incoming Links heading to obtain the location of the term within the Codification. Left-clicking the location will hyperlink to the Codification guidance.

FIGURE 1.8 | MASTER GLOSSARY SEARCH

Glossary

Use the quick find feature at the end of this page, or use the alphabetic index to browse the terms beginning with that letter.

> **General Note:** The Master Glossary contains all terms identified as glossary terms throughout the Codification. Clicking on any term in the Master Glossary will display where the term is used. The Master Glossary may contain identical terms with different definitions, some of which may not be appropriate for a particular Subtopic. For any particular Subtopic, users should only use the glossary terms included in the particular Subtopic Glossary Section (Section 20).

A | B | C | D | E | F | G | H | I | J | K | L | M | N | O | P | Q | R | S | T | U | V | W | X | Y | Z | 0-9 | View All

Glossary Term Quick Find

credit card fees

> **Credit Card Fees**
>
> INCOMING LINKS | USED IN TOPICS 310
>
> The periodic uniform fees that entitle cardholders to use credit cards. The amount of such fees generally is not dependent upon the level of credit available or frequency of usage. Typically the use of credit cards facilitates the cardholder's payment for the purchase of goods and services on a periodic, as-billed basis (usually monthly), involves the extension of credit, and, if payment is not made when billed, involves imposition of interest or finance charges. Credit card fees include fees received in similar arrangements, such as charge card and cash card fees.

FIGURE 1.9 MASTER GLOSSARY INCOMING LINKS

Glossary Term Usage

The glossary term is used in the following locations.

Credit Card Fees

310 Receivables > 20 Nonrefundable Fees and Other Costs > 05 Background
- 310 Receivables > 20 Nonrefundable Fees and Other Costs > 05 Background > General , paragraph 05-3

310 Receivables > 20 Nonrefundable Fees and Other Costs > 20 Glossary
- 310 Receivables > 20 Nonrefundable Fees and Other Costs > 20 Glossary

310 Receivables > 20 Nonrefundable Fees and Other Costs > 25 Recognition
- 310 Receivables > 20 Nonrefundable Fees and Other Costs > 25 Recognition > General , paragraph 25-1

310 Receivables > 20 Nonrefundable Fees and Other Costs > 35 Subsequent Measurement
- 310 Receivables > 20 Nonrefundable Fees and Other Costs > 35 Subsequent Measurement > General , paragraph 35-1

310 Receivables > 20 Nonrefundable Fees and Other Costs > 50 Disclosure
- 310 Receivables > 20 Nonrefundable Fees and Other Costs > 50 Disclosure > General , paragraph 50-4

EXAMPLE: NTT Inc. (NTT) issues credit cards to various target markets. NTT charges an annual fee for using the card as well as charging variable interest rates on outstanding balances exceeding 30 days. What are credit card fees?[4]

Discussion: Left-click the Master Glossary heading in the left navigation panel, and the alphabetic index and Glossary Term Quick Find options appear. Type in the term "credit card fees," as in Figure 1.8, and the definition in the bottom half of Figure 1.8 appears. To hyperlink to additional information related to credit card fees (Figure 1.9), left-click on the Incoming Links heading.

Topical Categories

As previously mentioned, the topical categories (Presentation, Assets, Liabilities, Equity, Revenue, Expenses, Broad Transactions, and Industry) are always displayed in the left navigation panel. Because most researchers have an idea of which topic is of interest to them, this tends to be the favorite search method and thus is utilized more than the other search functions. To search within the topics, move the cursor over the category of interest to open the subtopic window (see Figure 1.10). Keep moving the cursor to the right to open new windows until reaching the final area of interest, at which point left-clicking will allow access to the desired information in the center screen area.

EXAMPLE: NTT issues credit cards to various target markets. NTT charges an annual fee for using the card as well as charging variable interest rates on outstanding balances exceeding 30 days. How and when should NTT recognize the credit card fees?

Discussion: Credit card fees are receivables for the issuing company. As illustrated in Figure 1.13, highlight Assets and 310 – Receivables. At this point, a subtopic must be selected. Since the example concerns fees, it would seem that 20 – Nonrefundable Fees and Other Costs would be a likely choice. Left-click subtopic 20 to display its sections, as illustrated in part A of Figure 1.11. Because the example concerns recognition of credit card fees, sections 25 Recognition, 30 Initial Measurement, and 35 Subsequent Measurement are possibilities. However,

---

[4] Modified from the 2011 CPA Sample Exam.

after reexamining the question—not only *how*, but also *when* to recognize credit card fees, section 35 – Subsequent Measurement seems to be the best choice. Once in section 35, scroll down to paragraph 5 (ASC 310-20-35-5), as illustrated in part B of Figure 1.11. Once in this paragraph, left-click on the provided hyperlink (see part C of Figure 1.11) to verify the guidance pertains to credit card fees.

FIGURE 1.10 | TOPICAL CATEGORY SEARCH

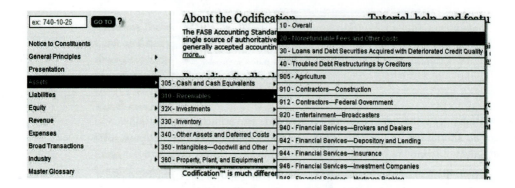

FIGURE 1.11 | SUBTOPICS AND SECTIONS

(A) Subtopic 20 Nonrefundable Fees and Other Costs

    ⊟   310 Receivables
        ⊟   20 Nonrefundable Fees and Other Costs
            ⊞ 00 Status
            ⊞ 05 Overview and Background
            ⊞ 15 Scope and Scope Exceptions
            ■ 20 Glossary
            ⊟ 25 Recognition
                ⊞ General
            ⊞ 30 Initial Measurement
            ⊞ 35 Subsequent Measurement
            ⊞ 40 Derecognition
            ⊞ 45 Other Presentation Matters
            ⊞ 50 Disclosure
            ⊞ 55 Implementation Guidance and Illustrations
            ⊞ 60 Relationships
            ■ 75 XBRL Elements

(B) Result from Clicking on Section

> **Credit Card Fees and Costs**

35-4   The following guidance addresses the amortization of deferred origination costs of credit cards with fees, without fees, or when the fees have been waived for a limited period of time.

35-5   Fees deferred in accordance with paragraph 310-20-25-15 shall be recognized on a straight-line basis over the period the fee entitles the cardholder to use the card. This accounting shall also apply to other similar card arrangements that involve an extension of credit by the card issuer.

(C) Result from Verifying Section

> **Credit Card Fees and Costs**

25-15   Credit card fees generally cover many services to cardholders. Accordingly, fees that are periodically charged to cardholders shall be deferred. This accounting shall also apply to other similar card arrangements that involve an extension of credit by the card issuer.

FIGURE 1.12	KEYWORD SEARCH

(A) Basic Keyword Search

(B) Basic Keyword Search Result

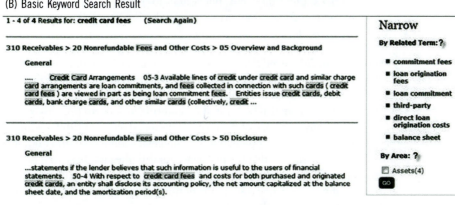

Keyword Search: Basic and Advanced

Basic A keyword search utilizes the Search bar appearing in the top right screen area of the database, as illustrated in part A of Figure 1.12. Enter a single keyword or multiple keywords and left-click the Go button. The search results appear in the center screen area with short excerpts under each heading. Left-click the desired heading to produce the related literature. Note that use of the Search bar results in the appearance of a box to the right of the results that helps narrow the search by related terms or by area.

> **EXAMPLE:** NTT issues credit cards to various target markets. NTT charges an annual fee for using the card as well as charging variable interest rates on outstanding balances exceeding 30 days. How and when should NTT recognize the credit card fees?

> **Discussion:** The question asks about credit card fees, a good starting point for a keyword search. As illustrated in part A of Figure 1.12, enter the term "credit card fees" in the Search bar in the top right screen area. After left-clicking the Go

button, the search results appear in the center screen area, as illustrated in part B of Figure 1.12. Additionally, a box appears to the right, suggesting options to narrow the search by related term or area. However, there are only four results from the search, so it will not be necessary to utilize that function. NTT is interested in *how* and *when* to recognize credit card fees. After examining the four search results, both ASC 310-20-25-1 and ASC 310-20-35-1 look appropriate. However, after reading the excerpts, it appears that section 25 examines how to recognize credit card fees (deferral), but not when to recognize these fees. ASC 310-20-35 (Subsequent Measurement) addresses both parts of the question, and, therefore, ASC 310-20-35-5 is the answer.

Advanced An Advanced Search option is located beneath the Search bar. As illustrated in Figure 1.13, this feature allows the search to include all areas in the Codification or to be narrowed to specific areas with topic/subtopic choices, as shown with the Revenue topic. The search can also be limited by entering a keyword (all, any word, exact phrase, or within so many words), Codification reference, document title/heading, area (all areas or specific areas without topic/subtopic choices), source type (the Codification or other), and number of results to display per page. As with the simple search function, the search terms appear in the center screen area, with a window to the right containing suggested narrowing subtopics. Once a search is performed, the Advanced Search option reappears below the potential results.

> **EXAMPLE:** NTT has entered into a lease transaction and has determined the lease qualifies as a capital lease. As the lessee, what amount should NTT initially recognize as the lease obligation?

FIGURE 1.13 | **ADVANCED KEYWORD SEARCH**

Advanced Search

Enter your search criteria in one or more of the fields that follow. Narrow your search by selecting specific Codification areas or document sources.

Narrow Search Area: ○ All areas ● Specific areas

- ⊞ ☐ General Principles
- ⊞ ☐ Presentation
- ⊞ ☐ Assets
- ⊞ ☐ Liabilities
- ⊞ ☐ Equity
- ⊟ ☐ Revenue
  - ⊞ ☐ 605 - Revenue Recognition
- ⊞ ☐ Expenses
- ⊞ ☐ Broad Transactions
- ⊞ ☐ Industry

Text/Keyword: [＿＿＿＿＿] **?**
● all ○ any word ○ exact phrase ○ within [＿] words

Codification Reference: [＿] – [＿] – [＿] **?**
Topic   Subtopic   Section

Document Title/Heading: [＿＿＿＿＿] **?**

Area: [All Areas ▼] **?**

Source Type: [Codification ▼] **?**

Results per page: [10 ▼]

Discussion: The question asks how to initially record a capital lease for a lessee. As illustrated in Figure 1.14, the Narrow Search Area in the Advanced Search is used first to limit results to the initial measurement of capital leases (ASC 840-30-30). When the keyword "lessee" is entered, only one result appears (ASC 840-30-30-1), as illustrated in Figure 1.15. Additionally, a box appears to the right, suggesting options to narrow the search by related term or area. For this example, it is not necessary, since there is only one result.

FIGURE 1.14	ADVANCED KEYWORD SEARCH—NARROWING THE SEARCH AREA

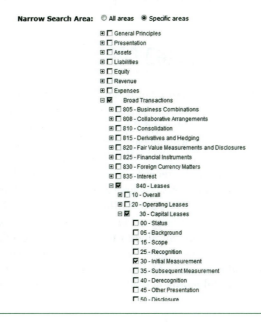

FIGURE 1.15	ADVANCED KEYWORD SEARCH—RESULT FOR LESSEES AFTER NARROWING THE SEARCH

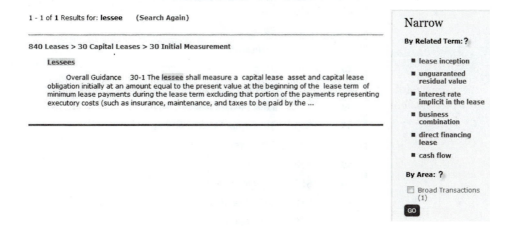

Moving within the Codification and Section Links

For all searches, use the back arrow in the browser to move back to the previous search. Alternatively, left-click on the larger topical area, and the previous search results will display. For instance, a search for "goodwill" results in the following topic and subtopic: 350-20 Intangibles – Goodwill and Other. A further refinement results in sections 05 Overview and Background and 15 Scope and Scope Exceptions. A researcher who left-clicks section 05 and then wants to return to the previous search results can either left-click the back arrow in the browser or left-click subtopic 20 to list all sections related to "goodwill."

Once in a content-related area, a box labeled Section Links appears at the bottom of the page along with a Page/Print Functions box. As illustrated in Figure 1.16, left-clicking on Section Links opens up a menu that allows the researcher to quickly link to related content.

EMAIL, PRINT, AND COPY/PASTE FUNCTIONS

The content of a standard can be emailed, printed, or copied and pasted. Once there is printable, content-related output, a Page/Print Functions box and an e-mail box will appear in a title bar at the bottom of the screen. Left-click on the heading, and as illustrated in Figure 1.17, a menu will appear. To email the content, simply left-click on the Email box and fill out the form appearing in Figure 1.18.

To print a particular record after a search has resulted in printable content, left-click the Page/Print Functions box appearing in the title bar at the bottom of the screen. A menu will appear, as previously illustrated in Figure 1.17. Choose Printer-Friendly to print or copy the record shown to another program. Choose Printer-Friendly with TOC to print or copy the content along with the associated table of contents. Choose Printer-Friendly with sources to print or copy the content along with the corresponding archived standard and references. Output from each of the print options appears in Figure 1.19. Selecting any of the print options opens a new window. Alternatively, the researcher can

---

FIGURE 1.16 | SECTION LINKS MENU

§ Section Links		ƒ Page / Print Functions
FASB	**SEC**	**Section**
00	S00	Status
05		Background
10		Objectives
15		Scope
20		Glossary
30		**Initial Measurement**
35	S35	Subsequent Measurement
45	S45	Other Presentation
50	S50	Disclosure
55	S55	Implementation
75	S75	XBRL Elements
	S99	SEC Materials

| FIGURE 1.17 | PAGE/PRINT FUNCTIONS MENU |

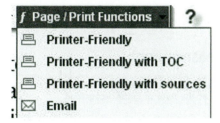

choose to print or copy the content of that window using the print or copy function within the browser. The copy function is explained in more detail below.

There are two approaches to copying a record. The first is to highlight the results from any of the search methods. Use the copy function within the browser and paste into another document either using the paste function within the location (Word, Excel) or right-clicking the mouse to use its paste function. This approach provides only the section and paragraph numbers, not the entire citation. Therefore, following the second approach is a better option. Select any of the print options from the Page/Print Functions menu discussed above. This will open a new window from which the researcher can copy and paste the entire output (including citation) using the mouse or the browser functions.

| FIGURE 1.18 | EMAIL OPTION |

Email a Colleague

Initial Measurement (330 > 10 > 30)

required fields marked with *

*Your Name: _____

*Your Email Address: _____
For return address purposes

*Email Address of Recipient(s): _____
Separate multiple addresses with commas

Message: _____
Optional

SUBMIT

FIGURE 1.19	PRINT OPTIONS

(A) Printer-Friendly Output

330 Inventory
10 Overall
30 Initial Measurement

General Note: The Initial Measurement Section provides guidance on the criteria and amounts used to measure a particular item at the date of initial recognition.

General

> **Cost Basis**

330-10-30-1 The primary basis of accounting for inventories is cost, which has been defined generally as the price paid or consideration given to acquire an asset. As applied to inventories, cost means in principle the sum of the applicable expenditures and charges directly or indirectly incurred in bringing an article to its existing condition and location. It is understood to mean acquisition and production cost, and its determination involves many considerations.

(B) Printer-Friendly with TOC Output

[330-10-30]   **Overall - Initial Measurement**
                     General
                        > Cost Basis
                        > Determination of Inventory Costs
                        > Consistency Required
                        > Purchases and Sales of Inventory with the Same Counterparty
                        > Costs Resulting from Share-Based Payment Transactions
                        > Costs of Computer Software to Be Sold, Leased, or Otherwise Marketed
                        > Costs of Certain Construction-Type and Production-Type Contracts

General Note: The Initial Measurement Section provides guidance on the criteria and amounts used to measure a particular item at the date of initial recognition.

General

> **Cost Basis**

330-10-30-1 The primary basis of accounting for inventories is cost, which has been defined generally as the price paid or consideration given to acquire an asset. As applied to inventories, cost means in principle the sum of the applicable expenditures and charges directly or indirectly incurred in bringing an article to its existing condition and location. It is understood to mean acquisition and production cost, and its determination involves many considerations.

| FIGURE 1.19 | PRINT OPTIONS (CONTINUED) |

(C) Printer-Friendly with Sources Output

330 Inventory
10 Overall
30 Initial Measurement

General Note: The Initial Measurement Section provides guidance on the criteria and amounts used to measure a particular item at the date of initial recognition.

General

> **Cost Basis**

330-10-30-1 [The primary basis of accounting for inventories is cost, which has been defined generally as the price paid or consideration given to acquire an asset. As applied to inventories, cost means in principle the sum of the applicable expenditures and charges directly or indirectly incurred in bringing an article to its existing condition and location. [ARB 43, paragraph Ch. 4 Statement 3, sequence 169]] [It is understood to mean acquisition and production cost, and its determination involves many considerations. [ARB 43, paragraph Ch. 4 Par. 5, sequence 170.1.2]]

SUMMARY

Accounting research is challenging because GAAP is based on fluid principles, reflecting current accounting thought that constantly changes via updates to the Codification. Although the Codification has consolidated GAAP down to two levels, there are still many sources one needs to examine (e.g., SEC pronouncements) as part of the research process. One needs to start with the Codification to find relevant authorities. Thus, one must understand the database's structure, its contents, and appropriate search techniques, including topical category searches, master glossary searches, and keyword searches. Since most users have an idea of the content area of interest, the topical category search is often the most practical starting point once in the Codification. For those familiar with superseded literature, the cross-reference function is a valuable tool. Practice developing research and analytical skills to meet the standards of the accounting profession and the public's expectations.

2 Electronic International Financial Reporting Standards

International competition has forced many firms to look to new markets to remain competitive. Increasingly internationalized capital markets result in a need for internationally comparable financial statements and accounting standards, thereby leading to efforts during the past decade to move nations toward using international standards. The movement toward harmonization and convergence[1] has included the activities of supranational groups and individual scholars. Figures 2.1[2] and 2.2[3] depict the global and U.S. International Financial Reporting Standards (IFRS) convergence efforts in recent years, respectively.

Research on accounting issues is conducted in a dynamic international environment. New professional standards are constantly issued. The updating of existing standards influenced by various constituents helps to minimize the differences across national boundaries. This chapter examines research in electronic IFRS (eIFRS).

IFRS RESEARCH

International accounting research takes place in a complex environment with numerous accounting standards, rules, and recommended practices. This chapter focuses solely on IFRS research. A sound understanding of the IFRS hierarchy and the eIFRS database is needed. The eIFRS database enables researchers to obtain authoritative evidence to help answer their research questions more efficiently than using bound books.

IFRS HIERARCHY

The International Accounting Standards Board (IASB) issues pronouncements labeled International Financial Reporting Standards (IFRSs). The IFRS Interpretations Committee issues interpretations of pronouncements known as IFRICs. The IASB also recognizes predecessor pronouncements and interpretations known as International Accounting Standards (IASs) and Standards Interpretations Committee interpretations (SICs), respectively. Collectively, all pronouncements and interpretations are known as the IFRS. A hierarchy exists among the standards issued within and related to the IFRS. This hierarchy shows the researcher where to begin the search for a solution to a problem or issue under review. Although all standards included in the IFRS (IFRSs, IFRICs, IASs, and SICs) have the same authority, IFRS *application* is hierarchical, and the researcher may find that an IFRS does not contain the needed information to address the

---

[1] Harmonization moves toward reducing the overall number of alternatives, but still allows for them as long as the alternatives do not conflict with the International Financial Reporting Standards. On the other hand, convergence moves toward adopting one set of standards.

[2] Developed from dates listed on the International Accounting Standards Board website, "IASB and the IASC Foundation: Who Are We and What Do We Do?" (www.iasb.org), and in "International Financial Reporting Standards (IFRS): An AICPA Backgrounder" (www.IFRS.com).

[3] Adapted from "International Financial Reporting Standards (IFRS): An AICPA Backgrounder" (www.IFRS.com).

FIGURE 2.1 GLOBAL IFRS TIME LINE

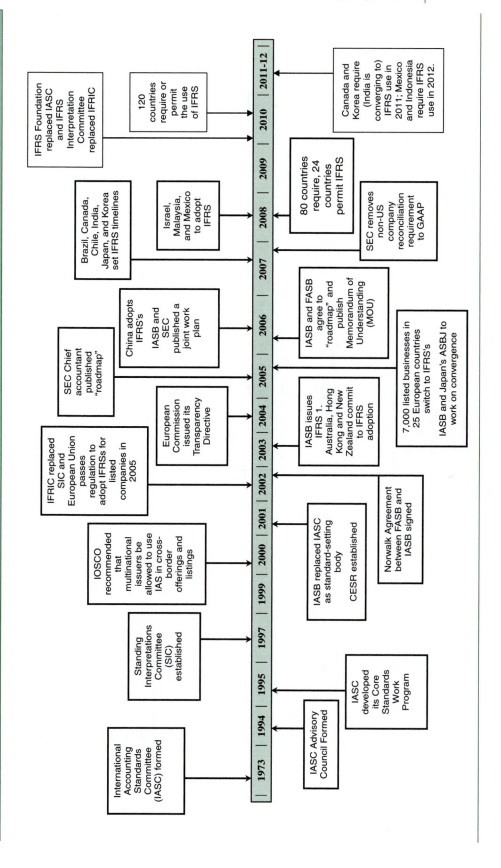

FIGURE 2.2 | U.S. IFRS TIME LINE

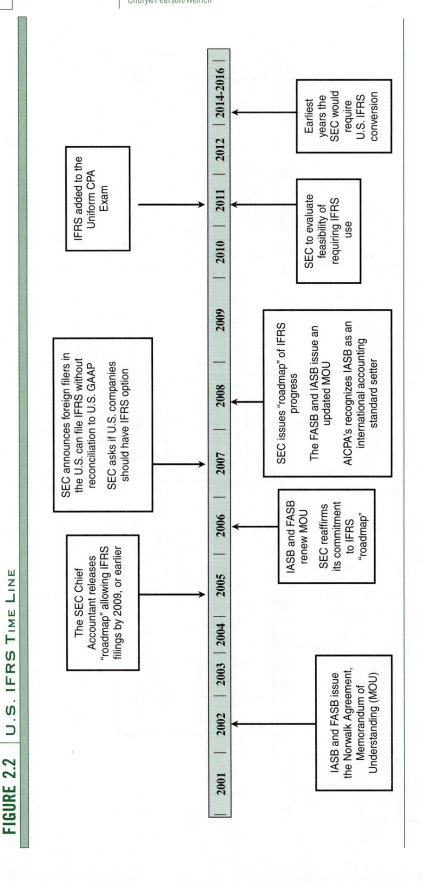

question. IAS No. 8, "Accounting Policies, Changes in Accounting Estimates and Errors," establishes a hierarchy for choosing IFRS accounting policies.

1. Apply the specific IFRS and consider relevant implementation guidance. If the specific IFRS does not resolve the issue, choose the relevant and reliable accounting policy from the listed sources in the following order:

    a. Apply other IFRSs that address similar or related issues.

    b. Apply the IASB Framework.

    c. Apply pronouncements of other standard-setting bodies that are consistent with the IASB Framework.

eIFRS ACCESS

There are several subscription services for eIFRS access available through the IASB and the International Association for Accounting Education and Research (IAAER). The IASB subscription can be accessed through the Products & services tab on the IASB home page, www.ifrs.org, as illustrated in part A of Figure 2.3. After left-clicking on the eIFRS heading, a log-in page appears (part B of Figure 2.3) with two options for subscribing to eIFRS.

1. The first option is to register for free enabling access to free content on the IFRS Foundation website. This option also allows the user to receive email alerts, access the unaccompanied standards, view IFRS for Small and Medium-Sized Entities (SMEs), register to observe meetings, and submit comment letters. Unaccompanied standards are the core standards in English without implementation guidance or bases for conclusions.

FIGURE 2.3 | eIFRS Access

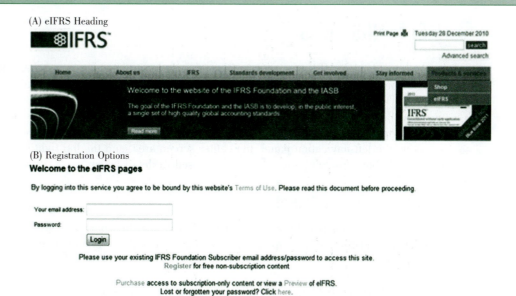

(A) eIFRS Heading

(B) Registration Options

FIGURE 2.4 | IAAER ACCESS

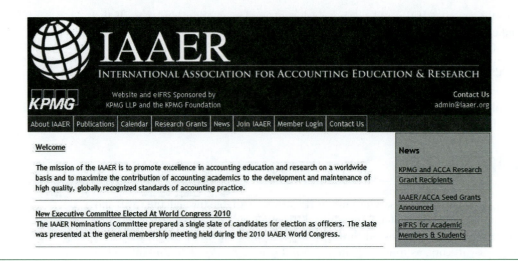

2. The second option is to purchase a subscription that includes online service with or without CD-ROMs and printed publications. At present, online IFRS access offers HTML versions of IFRSs in English and PDF versions of IFRSs in nine languages (English, German, Spanish, French, Greek, Dutch, Italian, Russian, and Slovak).

KPMG sponsors full access to the IASB's eIFRS online version for members of the IAAER (www.iaaer.org) (see Figure 2.4). Three subscriptions (individual, student, and university) are offered for varying rates (see Figure 2.5), and students joining the IAAER greatly benefit from low-cost access to this database. Note that this subscription requires logging into eIFRS through the IAAER member page.

ENTERING eIFRS

After logging into eIFRS (using any of the subscription options), the researcher is brought to a conditions of use page (Figure 2.6). From there, the researcher can click on the eIFRS heading to be brought to the opening screen of eIFRS (Figure 2.7). Note that, since the researcher is brought to the IFRS Foundation/IASB home page, the same seven tabs appear as in part A of Figure 2.3. The eIFRS home page is separated into three areas: the left navigation panel, the center screen area, and the top right screen area, located above the tabs. Each area is discussed in detail below.

Left Navigation Panel

The left navigation panel is split into three areas: Subcribers only, Registered users, and other information. The Registered users area is a limited version of the Subscribers only area.

Subscribers Only There are five items in the Subscribers only area: IFRSs (All Languages), IFRS for SMEs, Additional Material, Search, and Terminology.

FIGURE 2.5 | IAAER SUBSCRIPTION OPTIONS

INDIVIDUALS	<u>Join as an individual member</u> *One-year membership: US$25* Enjoy full, unlimited access to all eIFRSs! This includes the most up-to-date electronic html versions of all International Financial Reporting Standards including International Accounting Standards (IASs), Interpretations (IFRICs/SICs) and IASB-issued supporting documents-application guidance, illustrative examples, implementation guidance, bases for conclusions and all appendices. For a preview, visit <u>http://eifrs.iasb.org/eifrs/Preview</u>.
STUDENTS & PhD CANDIDATES	<u>Join as a student member or PhD candidate member</u> *One-year membership while enrolled: US$20* Download: <u>Student Membership Flyer</u> Enjoy full, unlimited access to all eIFRSs! This includes the most up-to-date electronic html versions of all International Financial Reporting Standards including International Accounting Standards (IASs), Interpretations (IFRICs/SICs) and IASB-issued supporting documents-application guidance, illustrative examples, implementation guidance, bases for conclusions and all appendices. For a preview, visit <u>http://eifrs.iasb.org/eifrs/Preview</u>.
UNIVERSITY MEMBERSHIP **(Universities & Colleges)**	<u>Join as a university member</u> *One-year membership: Varying rates* - Full, unlimited access to all eIFRSs hosted by the IASB. This includes the most up-to-date electronic html versions of all International Financial Reporting Standards including International Accounting Standards (IASs), Interpretations (IFRICs/SICs) and IASB-issued supporting documents-application guidance, illustrative examples, implementation guidance, bases for conclusions and all appendices. For a preview, visit <u>http://eifrs.iasb.org/eifrs/Preview</u>. - The IAAER website provides a link to all University members' websites and also enables search-engine support through the IFAC web search located at the bottom of each webpage.

FIGURE 2.6 | CONDITIONS OF USE

<u>Update Profile</u>   <u>Change Password</u>   <u>Logout</u>

After clicking on the link below, if you are prompted to log in by eIFRS, please enter your IAAER username and password to successfully log in to eIFRS.

<u>*eIFRS (electronic* International Financial Reporting Standards)</u>
International Accounting Standards Board

By clicking on the above link, you are agreeing to the following terms & conditions of use:

- eIFRS access is restricted to academic members of the IAAER.
- The service takes the form of direct access to the IASB's online database service of International Financial Reporting Standards and related information.
- Members may reproduce works in unaltered form for personal, non-commercial use subject to the inclusion of an acknowledgement of IASCF's copyright in the works.
- Members may not reproduce in either hardcopy or electronic format the text of any individual standard or specific document, extract or combination thereof of the works for any seminar, conference, training or similar commercial event.
- Members are obligated to obtain the approval from the IASCF to use the Works for commercial purposes or public distribution.

| FIGURE 2.7 | eIFRS Opening Screen |

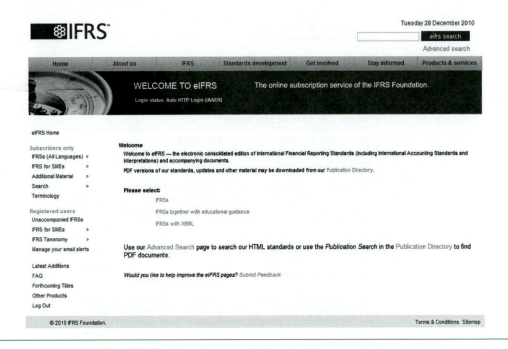

1. IFRSs (All Languages)—provides access to the standards in HTML (English only) and PDF (all available languages). Choosing the HTML option allows the researcher to select between the latest published standards and the Advanced search option to be discussed later. The latest published standards are an electronic version of the annual hardbound consolidated collections issued by the IASB, including the Framework; the standards (IFRSs, IFRICs, IASs, and SICs); a glossary; due process handbooks for the IASB, the IFRIC, and the Foundation; and the Constitution (original, revised, and Part 2). Additionally, the collections include a table of contents, preface, and introduction for the IFRS; a presentation of financial statements; an expert advisory panel statement on measuring fair value; and a judgment statement on measuring fair value.

2. IFRS for SMEs—provides access to the standard in HTML (English only) and PDF (English and six other languages). The IFRS for SMEs is a single standard that contains less than 250 pages and is less complex than full IFRSs due to option simplifications and fewer disclosure requirements. Left-clicking on this heading provides links to illustrative financial statements, a table of contents, an introduction, the standard for SMEs, an appendix, board approval, the basis for conclusions, and a glossary.

3. Additional Material—provides access to editorial corrections, educational material, IFRIC updates, IASB updates, IASB Insight, IFRIC drafts, exposure drafts, discussion papers, near final drafts, IFRIC due process, revised standards, and versions in six other languages besides English.

4. Search—provides access to an advanced HTML search or a PDF publication search. This will be discussed in detail later in the chapter.

5. Terminology—provides a link to a terminology lookup with approximately 1,500 terms. Terms can be searched in twenty-one languages. This feature will be discussed in detail later in the chapter.

Registered Users The Registered users area is a limited version of the Subscribers only area and contains four items.

1. Unaccompanied IFRSs—provides a link in English to the current year's core standards (without implementation guidance or bases for conclusions) and IFRS for SMEs.
2. IFRS for SMEs—provides access in eight languages to the standard, basis for conclusion, and illustrative financial statements.
3. IFRS Taxonomy—provides PDF access to full IFRSs, ordered by standard or report, and IFRS for SMEs.
4. Manage your email alerts—provides options for email notifications.

Other Information This area contains links to the latest additions (the ten most recent files that have been published); four frequently asked questions (FAQ) (covering subscriptions, log-ins, technical service, and access problems), forthcoming titles with notification of availability links, and links to partner publications.

Center Screen Area

The center screen starts with a welcome message and provides access to IFRSs, IFRSs together with educational guidance, IFRSs with XBRL, and the advanced search page to be discussed later in the chapter.

1. Left-clicking on the IFRSs heading provides access to collections from January 2005 to the present. Most collections provide both HTML and PDF versions. Links to non–English language versions and the advanced search are also provided.
2. Left-clicking on the IFRSs together with educational guidance heading provides access to HTML volumes from 2007 to the present. The educational volumes contain (in green italics) cross-references and footnotes developed by the IFRS Foundation education staff. For instance, when examining the objective for IFRS 3, "Business Combinations," the researcher sees green italicized links to the glossary (G) and to other paragraphs (paragraphs 10–31). The educational guidance is not part of the IFRS. As with the IFRS search, there is a link to the Advanced search option.
3. Left-clicking on the IFRS with XBRL heading provides access to xIFRS (IFRSs and IASs with XBRL) and IFRS for SMEs with XBRL. xIFRS is a tool to aid in viewing and understanding the IFRS taxonomy (see Figure 2.8).

FIGURE 2.8 | XBRL TAXONOMY

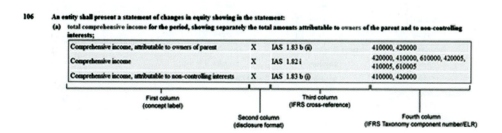

Top Right Screen Area

The top right screen area contains two options, an eIFRS search that produces PDF/Word documents related to the search term and an advanced search. Both are discussed in detail in the next section.

IFRS RESEARCH PROCESS

Search processes in eIFRS include using terminology lookup, searching the glossary, directly searching for a desired standard through collections/volumes found in IFRSs or IFRSs together with educational content, using a basic search inquiry, and using an advanced search inquiry. Each search process is located in multiple locations; however, access to each search process (except the glossary) is always available through the left navigation panel or the top right screen area, as previously referenced in Figure 2.7, the eIFRS opening screen. Each search process is discussed in detail below.

1. The first method for searching eIFRS uses the terminology lookup, which contains approximately 1,500 key IFRS terms. As illustrated in Figure 2.9, the researcher has the option of searching in thirty different languages (source language) and the option of displaying the result in thirty different languages (target language). The search result provides a definition of the term, the standard and paragraph number in which the term is referenced, and a list of similar terms. The researcher may need to left-click on one of the similar terms in order to narrow the search term.

FIGURE 2.9 | TERMINOLOGY LOOKUP

Terminology Lookup

This tool searches approximately 1,500 key terms used in the official translations of the International Financial Reporting Standards. This terminology has been reviewed by a committee of accounting experts in each language. Languages are updated as and when changes are made. Please click here for more information on when each language was last updated.

Source Term:
Term: [   ]   Source Language: English ▾

Target Language(s): [select all] [clear]

Arabic: ☐	Bulgarian: ☐	Czech: ☐
Danish: ☐	German: ☐	Greek: ☐
English: ☐	Spanish: ☐	Estonian: ☐
Finnish: ☐	French: ☐	Hungarian: ☐
Italian: ☐	Japanese: ☐	Korean: ☐
Lithuanian: ☐	Latvian: ☐	Macedonian: ☐
Maltese: ☐	Dutch: ☐	Polish: ☐
Portuguese: ☐	Portuguese (Brazilian): ☐	Romanian: ☐
Slovak: ☐	Slovenian: ☐	Swedish: ☐
Turkish: ☐	Ukrainian: ☐	Chinese (Simplified): ☐
Chinese (Traditional): ☐		

[Find Terms]

FIGURE 2.10 | TERMINOLOGY LOOKUP SEARCH

(A) Other Similar Terms

Terminology Lookup

1: **Impairment**

Other similar terms:
*Property, Plant and Equipment - Compensation for the Impairment or Loss of Items *
evidence of impairment
Impairment loss
Impairment of Assets
Impairment test
Indicator [of impairment]
Interim Financial Reporting and Impairment
Tests goodwill for impairment

(B) Definition

Terminology Lookup

1: **Impairment loss**

The amount by which the carrying amount of an asset exceeds its recoverable amount. IAS 16.6, (IAS 36.6), IAS 38.8

EXAMPLE: NTT Inc. (NTT) is traded on an exchange and must follow the IFRS for financial reporting purposes. The company is required to examine tangible and intangible assets for impairment. How is impairment defined?

Discussion: Left-click the Terminology heading in the left navigation panel, bringing up the Technology Lookup screen, as illustrated in Figure 2.9 . Type in the term "impairment," bringing up a list of other similar research terms that can be used to narrow the search (see part A of Figure 2.10). Because the example is concerned with the term "impairment loss," left-click on that heading. The definition (along with the related standards) appears as illustrated in part B of Figure 2.10.

2. Once one enters the IFRS, a glossary is available by left-clicking on the IFRSs (All Languages) heading in the left navigation panel. Scroll down to just below the last standard and left-click on the Glossary heading. An alphabetical list of all referenced IFRS terms appears, along with a hyperlink to the related standard and paragraph, as illustrated in Figure 2.11.

3. The third method of searching eIFRS is to go directly to the desired section by left-clicking on the standard once in IFRSs or IFRSs together with educational guidance.

FIGURE 2.11 | GLOSSARY EXCERPT

accounting policies	The specific principles, bases, conventions, rules and practices applied by an entity in preparing and presenting financial statements.	IAS 8.5
accounting profit	Profit or loss for a period before deducting tax expense.	IAS 12.5
accrual basis of accounting	The effects of transactions and other events are recognised when they occur (and not as cash or its equivalent is received or paid) and they are recorded in the accounting records and reported in the financial statements of the periods to which they relate.	F.22

EXAMPLE: NTT is traded on an exchange and must follow the IFRS for financial reporting purposes. The company needs to determine how to value year-end inventory. Which standard provides this information?

Discussion: Left-click the IFRSs heading in the left navigation panel. A list of all IFRSs appears, as illustrated in part A of Figure 2.12. Scroll down until reaching the standard of interest (IAS 2). Left-click on the IAS 2 heading to reveal its contents (part B of Figure 2.12), and then left-click on the IAS 2 Inventories heading in the contents. Paragraph 1 (part C of Figure 2.12) explains the objectives of the standard and alludes to writing inventory down to net realizable value. Continue to scroll down to find out how to calculate net realizable value (paragraphs 6–7 and 28–33).

FIGURE 2.12 | INVENTORY SEARCH DIRECTLY ACCESSING STANDARDS

(A) Partial List of IFRSs

eIFRSs at 1 July 2010

Document
Contents
Preface to IFRS
Framework for the Preparation and Presentation of Financial Statements
Introduction to this edition
Presentation of Financial Statements
IFRS 1 First-time Adoption of International Financial Reporting Standards
IFRS 2 Share-based Payment
IFRS 3 Business Combinations
IFRS 4 Insurance Contracts
IFRS 5 Non-current Assets Held for Sale and Discontinued Operations
IFRS 6 Exploration for and Evaluation of Mineral Resources
IFRS 7 Financial Instruments: Disclosures
IFRS 8 Operating Segments
IFRS 9 Financial Instruments
IAS 1 Presentation of Financial Statements
IAS 2 Inventories
IAS 7 Statement of Cash Flows

(B) IAS 2 Components

Search Results

eIFRSs at 1 July 2010

Document	Date of Issue
IAS 2 Contents	
IAS 2 Introduction	
IAS 2 Inventories	2004-03-31
IAS 2 Appendix Amendments to other pronouncements	
IAS 2 Approval by the Board of IAS 2 issued in December 2003	
IAS 2 Basis for Conclusions	

(C) Screenshot after Clicking on IAS 2 Inventories Heading

1   The objective of this Standard is to prescribe the accounting treatment for inventories. A primary issue in accounting for inventories is the amount of cost to be recognised as an asset and carried forward until the related revenues are recognised. This Standard provides guidance on the determination of cost and its subsequent recognition as an expense, including any write-down to net realisable value. It also provides guidance on the cost formulas that are used to assign costs to inventories.

4. A fourth search method within eIFRS uses the eIFRS search bar, located in the top right screen area. This method returns PDF or Word documents that have the search term in their title only. The documents are not searchable through eIFRS functions and do not contain links to the search term located within the document. Therefore, the researcher will want to access the Advanced Search option, which provides searchable links, including highlighted search terms.

5. The fifth search method within eIFRS, the Advanced Search option (illustrated in Figure 2.13), can be accessed from multiple locations (the Search subcomponent of the left navigation panel, the center screen area, and the top right screen area). The researcher can refine a search by collection, standard issuance date, educational material, exact text, relative importance of words by using the $>$ and $<$ symbols,

---

FIGURE 2.13 | ADVANCED SEARCH FUNCTION

(A) Screenshot of Advanced Search

Advanced Search
All fields are optional

Collection	eIFRSs at 1 July 2010 ▼
Education Material	☐
Text	LIFO Exact Text? ☑ Sort by relevance ☐ (tips)
Highlight Terms?	☑
Standard	All ▼
Issued [YYYY-MM-DD]	___ to ___ (Standards only)

[Search]

Search Tips for Text search (applicable to non-exact:match searches only)

- Enclose phrases in "double quotes"
- Sort by relevance only applicable when 'text' is used also
- Use '+' to indicate words, phrases or groups that must be present
- Use '>' to indicate important words
- Use '<' to indicate less important words
- Use '*' to indicate extensions to a word ie - 'financ*' matches 'financial', 'finance' and 'finances'
- Use '(' and ')' to group sub-expressions
- Searches are case-insensitive

(B) LIFO Search Results

Search Results

eIFRSs at 1 July 2010

Document	Date of Issue
IAS 2 Introduction	
IAS 2 Basis for Conclusions	
IAS 19 Employee Benefits	2004-12-16
IAS 19 Basis for Conclusions	

(C) LIFO Use

Prohibition of LIFO as a cost formula

IN13   The Standard does not permit the use of the last-in, first-out (LIFO) formula to measure the cost of inventories.

BC9   The combination of the previous version of IAS 2 and SIC-1 *Consistency☐Different Cost Formulas for Inventories* allowed some choice between first-in, first-out (FIFO) or weighted average cost formulas (benchmark treatment) and the last-in, first-out (LIFO) method (allowed alternative treatment). The Board decided to eliminate the allowed alternative of using the LIFO method.

exact phrases by using quotations, or word stems by using the * symbol. The output can be refined by choosing to sort by relevance or by highlighting the search term. Choosing to highlight the search term is extremely beneficial, since searches can return entire standards.

EXAMPLE: NTT, a U.S.-based company, is considering expanding into the U.K. market and would like to buy an already established business there. NTT uses the last-in, first-out (LIFO) cost-flow method for inventory purposes. Will that inventory method be permitted in the United Kingdom?

Discussion: Left-click on the Search heading in the left navigation panel and choose Advanced Search, or left-click on the Advanced search heading in the top right screen area. As illustrated in part A of Figure 2.13, choose the most recent collection, type in "LIFO," and check the Highlight Terms? box. A list of all IFRSs related to LIFO appears, as illustrated in part B of Figure 2.13. Left-click on the first option (IAS 2 Introduction), and scroll down until finding the term "LIFO." Paragraph 13, as illustrated in part C of Figure 2.13, reveals that LIFO is not permitted under the IFRS. By also left-clicking on the second option (IAS 2 Basis for Conclusions) and scrolling down to the term "LIFO," one sees in Basis for Conclusions (BC) 9 that the IASB eliminated the LIFO method.

In deciding when to stop the research, consider the IFRS hierarchy. IFRSs, IFRICs, IASs, and SICs are primary authorities. If needed, use the Framework and other national GAAP in combination with other supporting authorities to address the research question when an answer does not exist within the highest levels of the IFRS.

Print and Copy/Paste Functions

eIFRS does not contain special print or copy/paste functions. The researcher can conveniently use the browser's print and copy/paste functions to export results from eIFRS searches.

SUMMARY

This chapter has presented an overview of the IFRS research process. Because the IFRS Foundation's objectives include promoting a single set of high-quality standards and promoting convergence, the IFRS is continuing to evolve. The research process may involve judgment because the IFRS employs a more principle-based approach than does, for instance, U.S. GAAP. Additionally, although all IFRSs are equal, the researcher must follow a hierarchy when a specific IFRS does not address the research question. If the researcher is familiar with the research topic, the most expeditious way to find a solution may be to examine the list of published IFRSs. For a comprehensive list of literature referencing a term or topic, the researcher wants to use a keyword search utilizing the option to highlight terms. The IASB is working independently and on joint projects with various international standard-setting bodies. Therefore, accountants must research changes in pronouncements to keep abreast of current applications of principles.

Other Research Databases

This chapter presents four databases used for financial accounting research: RIA Checkpoint, EDGAR, NetAdvantage, and LexisNexis Academic.

RIA CHECKPOINT (FINANCIAL LIBRARY)

RIA Checkpoint's financial library provides authoritative statements and insightful interpretations of GAAP, SEC rules, and other U.S. and international accounting and auditing standards. It is a commercial accounting database used to enhance the effectiveness and efficiency of accounting standards research. Commercial accounting databases have the advantage of providing access to both authoritative and nonauthoritative financial accounting standards and literature. Reference materials are provided throughout RIA Checkpoint and include commentary and interpretive guides from financial reporting experts. The database highlights key developments, new authorities, and proposals from the SEC, FASB, IASB, and other standard-setters.

RIA Checkpoint's opening research screen for the Accounting, Auditing, and Corporate Finance Library is shown in Figure 3.1. The database simply alphabetizes items under Standards and Regulations. Novice researchers must remember that authoritative U.S. GAAP comes only from the Codification. For instance, accounting standards that were set by the AICPA years ago are no longer current authoritative U.S. GAAP, since they have been superseded by the Codification.

In drilling down in RIA Checkpoint's access to the Codification, one finds other materials, such as exposure drafts, the master glossary, and accounting standards updates. FASB's superseded materials can be obtained from the FASB website. RIA Checkpoint's sources for international accounting information are shown in Figure 3.2. Note that, in addition to the standards and interpretations for IFRSs, proposal stage documents are included.

Various other libraries also exist in RIA Checkpoint. The SEC reference library is essential for those seeking to apply GAAP to public companies. The SEC library is divided into SEC Rules and Regulations, interpretations and guidance, forms, and other items. The interpretations and guidance section includes such issuances as financial reporting releases and staff accounting bulletins (SABs) that present the SEC's staff interpretations of financial accounting–related disclosure practices. Recall that the FASB's Codification includes only selective SEC materials.

One can search the RIA Checkpoint database by drilling down through the table of contents, using FASB cross-references, or conducting keyword searches. An index of accounting topics provides a backup search technique. The Find by Citation search option is displayed in Figure 3.3. RIA Checkpoint also provides information on current events in accounting.

FIGURE 3.1 | RIA CHECKPOINT'S OPENING RESEARCH SCREEN

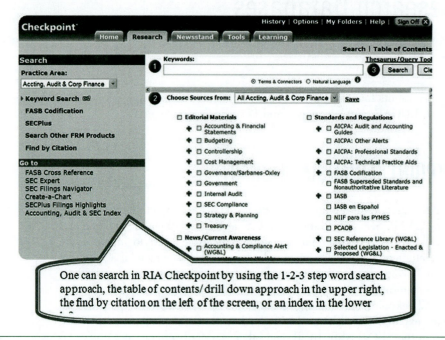

FIGURE 3.2 | IASB RELEASES IN RIA CHECKPOINT

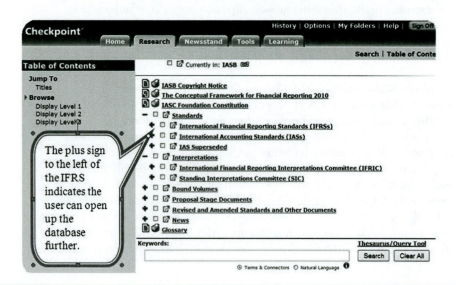

FIGURE 3.3 | EXAMPLE OF FIND BY CITATION IN RIA CHECKPOINT

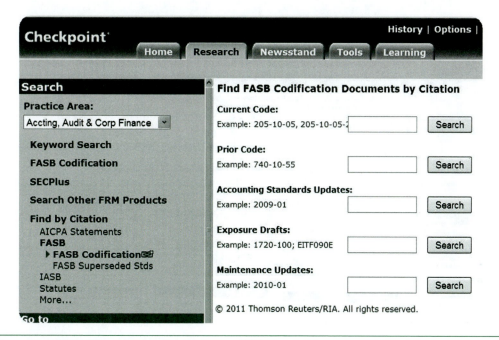

SEC's EDGAR DATABASE

Corporate filings with the SEC are accessed by using EDGAR (available through SEC's website. www.sec.gov). Corporate filings include 10-Ks, containing audited annual financial statements; 10-Qs, containing unaudited quarterly financial statements; 8-Ks, containing current information including preliminary earnings announcements; and many other types of documents. Alternatively, some commercial financial databases and many corporate websites provide similar access to filing information. However, sometimes there is no substitute for examining a company's 10-K (e.g., to read important footnote information and management's discussion and analysis of such topics as legal risks).

EDGAR allows the users (analysts, investors, and students) to extract data from corporate filings using customized searches. In EDGAR, one can search by company or fund name, ticker symbol, location, Standard Industrial Classification (SIC) code, and other methods. Figure 3.4 shows the opening screen of the SEC website and how to access EDGAR, either by using the Search function or by drilling down through Filings & Forms. Figure 3.5 shows the choices in EDGAR under Filings & Forms. One can also use EDGAR to search for mutual funds as well as their key disclosures and voting records.

Search limitations in EDGAR, as explained by the SEC, include the lack of notice that a specific filing was amended or withdrawn, the need to search for a company name as it is provided in SEC reports, and "the inability to compare the disclosures within specific filings (SEC)." For example, "[i]n certain instances, where a company's name includes a first and last name, such as "John Deere", you may have to search for "Deere John . . . ."

FIGURE 3.4 | SEC's EDGAR Database Opening Screen

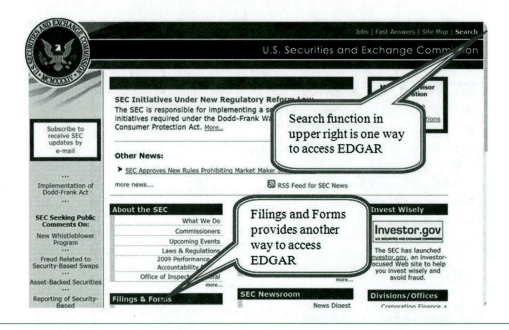

FIGURE 3.5 | SEC's EDGAR Database Screen for Filings & Forms

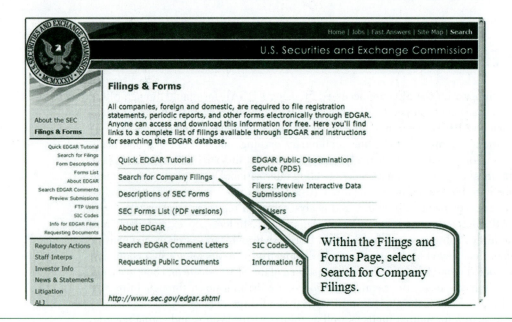

A company search in EDGAR is displayed in Figure 3.6 . Also, note that not all exhibits identified in a filing may be available through the search result that you are reviewing. This is because exhibits may be "incorporated by reference" when the issuer filed them with earlier SEC filings.

FIGURE 3.6 | SEC's EDGAR DATABASE RESULTS PAGE ON DELL

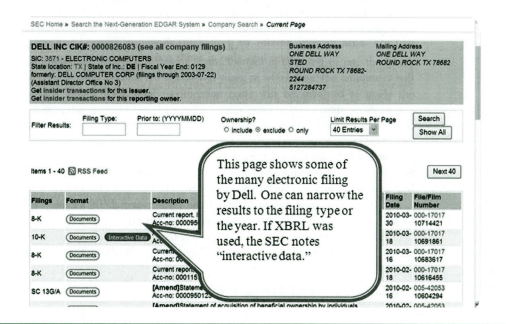

The SEC explains that it "is committed to transforming the EDGAR database from a form-based electronic filing cabinet to a dynamic real-time search tool with interactive capabilities using XBRL (SEC)." XBRL filings enable an investment analyst to extract specific data for analysis directly from filings without having to retype it. Notice that interactive data appear for the 10-K as shown in Figure 3.7.

FIGURE 3.7 | SEC's EDGAR DATABASE SHOWING XBRL DATA

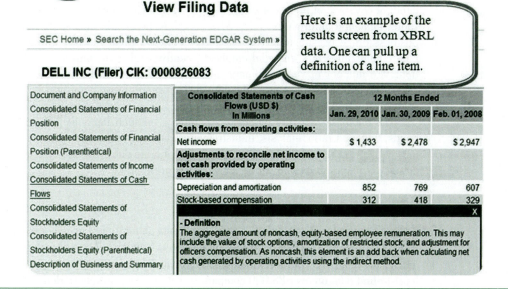

To enhance EDGAR's ease of use and utility, the SEC provides a quick tutorial as well as a guide that includes frequently asked questions (FAQ). For instance, one FAQ is whether one can search the EDGAR database for companies by state. The answer is yes: "Simply use the EDGAR Company Search and type in the state you want in the appropriate box." Since the passage of the Sarbanes–Oxley Act of 2002, an issuer must include certifications from its chief executive officer (CEO) and chief financial officer (CFO) concerning the accuracy of its Form 10-K (and Form 10-Q as well). These certifications (the certifications required by Sections 302 and 906) generally are attached to the filings as Exhibits 31 and 32.

The guide also provides some helpful search advice. For example, one should check to see if an amended version of a filing exists, shown by "/A." In EDGAR, one can find companies within an industry that have been assigned a specific SIC code. Use the SIC field in the EDGAR Company Search or in the Advanced Search option of the Full-Text Search. One can also limit search results to certain form types filed by a specific company by using the Companies and Other Filers Search. One can also narrow a search by year.

Some private companies build upon EDGAR's system. For example, I-Matrix provides a "suite of interactive data and analytical tools that provide quick and accurate XBRL-tagged financial statement data via Microsoft Excel® and an easy to use web interface." These add-ons to EDGAR are generally available only through paid subscriptions.

FINANCIAL RESEARCH DATABASES

Financial research databases include such databases as Standard and Poor's (S&P) NetAdvantage and LexisNexis Academic. These databases summarize and analyze various aspects of corporate filings with the SEC. For example, the financial statements from 10-Ks are summarized by these databases. The financial research databases attempt to add value by sometimes providing analysts' reports on a business and financial ratio analyses.

Financial analysis often examines the profitability, liquidity, and solvency of a company in order to determine its financial health. The importance of the financial analysis is shown in some of the cases explored in later chapters. Be cognizant that different databases sometimes generate different results for the same financial ratio on the same company for the same year.

Data and information are widely available for U.S. public companies. However, the depth of coverage of these companies varies by database. For example, some databases show segmental information on public company financials and such other items as business property, subsidiaries, long-term debt, and bond ratings. Initial searches of public companies in a financial database usually result in summary financial information. The number of years of financial information that can be viewed in a database varies, with three to five years being typical. This enables one to perform a trend analysis to determine the direction for change.

Some databases provide better access to data on such items as private companies, bonds, financial ratio analysis, industry comparisons of companies, and foreign companies. Other databases may excel in historical corporate data, investment analyst reports, corporate histories, mutual funds, or financial press news.

S&P NetAdvantage

S&P NetAdvantage markets itself as "a comprehensive source of business and investment information, offering on-line access to Standard & Poor's independent research, data and commentary on stocks, bonds, funds, and industries." The database includes hard-to-find data on over 85,000 companies that are not publicly traded. Because these private companies are not listed on a stock exchange, they do not need to file with the SEC.

Most of the opening screen features separate news on the market, bonds, the economy, and industries. The right side of the opening screen has quick links to industry surveys, investment publications, investment advisory reports, and S&P indices. Investment publications include bond reports, fund reports, security dealers, and others shown in the drop-down box. The bottom right of the opening screen provides a handful of guides on using the database.

An example of an S&P index is the S&P 500, which represents stocks selected by S&P as leading companies in various industries. The S&P 500 is often used as a benchmark for judging money managers. From the S&P NetAdvantage overview of the S&P 500, one is provided with various choices on the left side of the screen, such as viewing S&P 500 vital statistics.

S&P NetAdvantage also provides information on public companies, market news, investment analysts' reports, industry surveys, and more, as shown in its opening screen. The database includes a dozen financial and investment publications that provide insight for company research and analysis, such as the *Bond Guide*, *Mutual Fund Report*, *Dividend Record*, and *S&P's Corporation Records*. Use the tabs near the top of the screen in S&P NetAdvantage to go to the type of investment at issue, such as company research.

Powerful search and comparison functions exist in S&P NetAdvantage, allowing searches across multiple databases simultaneously to identify companies that meet specific criteria for analysis. Thus, S&P NetAdvantage can compare companies in different lines of business. Select from hundreds of database reports and charts. Make comparisons within the industry by choosing from various comparative reports. Use the North American Industrial Classification System (NAICS) code to identify competitors within the industry. Find statistics for companies in the S&P NetAdvantage portfolio. Create public information books to customize the content desired in a report.

Bond information is available in S&P NetAdvantage in spreadsheet format. The descriptive information on each bond includes the type of bond issuance, its rating, and whether it is callable. The numerical data usually include coupon rate, yield to maturity, sales price, and more.

EXAMPLE: Examine the bonds for General Motors (GM) to determine to what extent bondholders can convert to equity.

Discussion: On the right side of the opening screen, go to the drop-down box for Publication and select Bond Report. In the search drop-down box, type in the ticker (stock market abbreviation "GM," or change from ticker to company name and type in "General Motors." Select the arrow across to execute the search. Examine the spreadsheet information, looking primarily under the "callable" column. One can acquire additional information about the particular bond, such as a chart of the bond as compared to the S&P index for bonds, the issuance profile, key statistics, and the name of the underwriter.

LexisNexis Academic

LexisNexis Academic is a limited version of LexisNexis, a database that markets itself as providing "the most expansive collection of online content available anywhere." LexisNexis Academic markets itself as providing "a full range of credible sources for business information, including business and financial news, U.S. and international company financial information from government or private sources, market research,

FIGURE 3.8 | LEXISNEXIS ACADEMIC RATIO ANALYSIS ILLUSTRATED

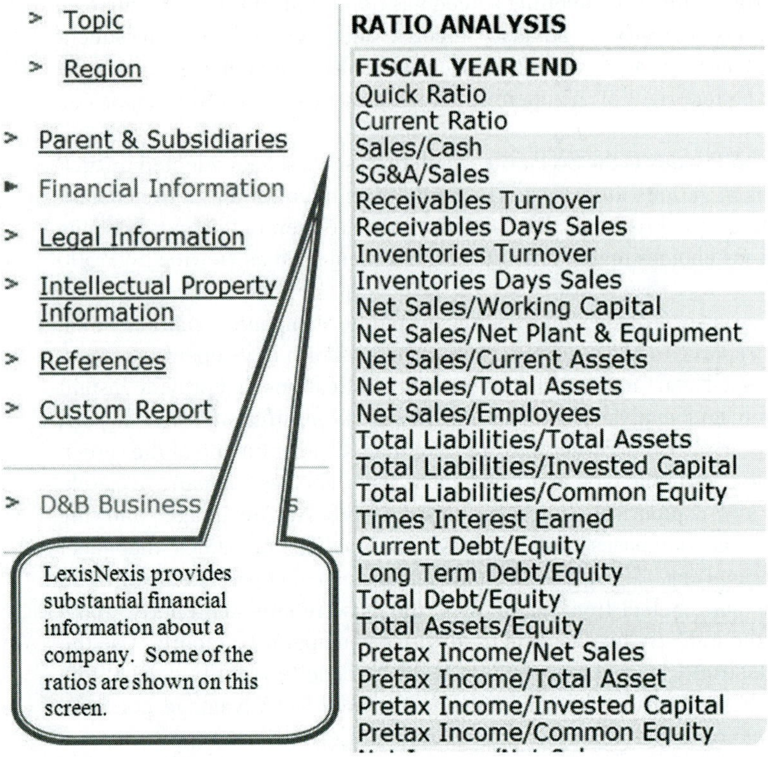

> Topic

> Region

> Parent & Subsidiaries

► Financial Information

> Legal Information

> Intellectual Property
  Information

> References

> Custom Report

> D&B Business

RATIO ANALYSIS

FISCAL YEAR END
Quick Ratio
Current Ratio
Sales/Cash
SG&A/Sales
Receivables Turnover
Receivables Days Sales
Inventories Turnover
Inventories Days Sales
Net Sales/Working Capital
Net Sales/Net Plant & Equipment
Net Sales/Current Assets
Net Sales/Total Assets
Net Sales/Employees
Total Liabilities/Total Assets
Total Liabilities/Invested Capital
Total Liabilities/Common Equity
Times Interest Earned
Current Debt/Equity
Long Term Debt/Equity
Total Debt/Equity
Total Assets/Equity
Pretax Income/Net Sales
Pretax Income/Total Asset
Pretax Income/Invested Capital
Pretax Income/Common Equity

LexisNexis provides substantial financial information about a company. Some of the ratios are shown on this screen.

industry reports, and actual SEC filings." The database describes itself as "one of the most heavily used databases in higher education.

The opening screen provides research tools for news, legal cases, corporations, countries, and people. Thus, in the opening screen, for example, one can search for Chevron's financials. The results are shown in Figure 3.8. The search defaults to the company dossier part of the database, which attempts to provide "a complete picture of a company's structure, financial health, brands and competitors."

Search results for a company will first present snapshot information. The snapshot provides contact information (such as address and website address), industry classification, business description, and current news. The snapshot's financial information includes a yearly financial summary (net income, net sales, total assets, and total liabilities), current stock quotes and charts for the past year, and stock outstanding. The people and firms listed in the snapshot are major executives, members of the board of directors, key competitors, legal counsel, and the auditor. For example, the opening screen results of a search for Dell's filings are shown in Figure 3.9.

Important additional selections that provide more detail on the company appear at the left side of the snapshot screen of the company dossier. In addition to the snapshot report just described, the database provides standard reports on press releases, parent and subsidiaries, financial information, legal information, intellectual property information, and references. Custom reports that combine parts of the snapshot and financial information pages can be generated.

FIGURE 3.9 | LexisNexis Academic Opening Screen on Dell

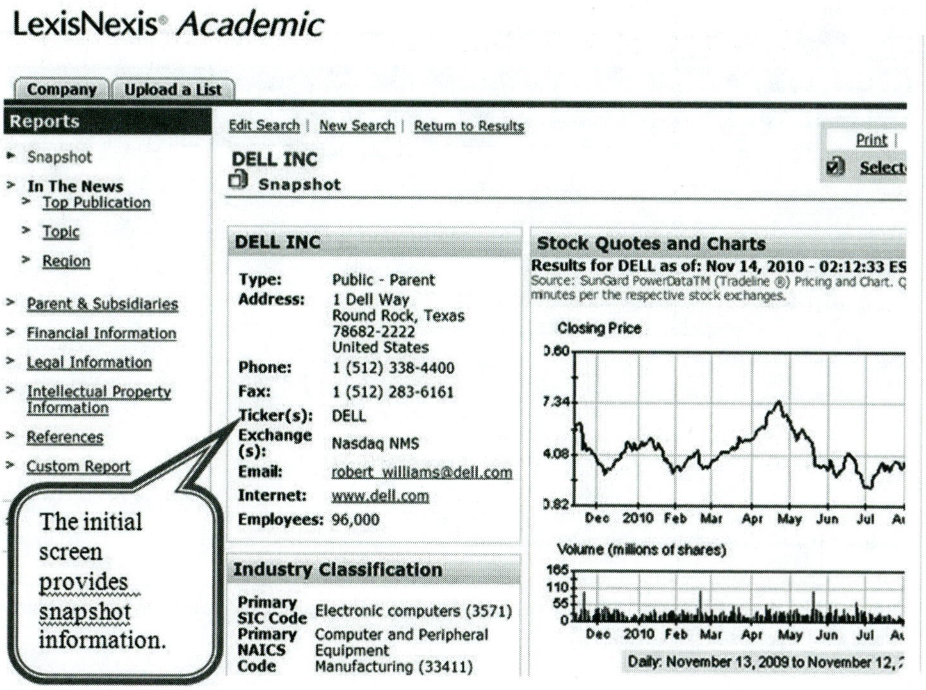

The initial screen provides snapshot information.

Selecting the Financial Information option brings up five years' worth of sales data, net income, and sometimes earnings per share data. Annual figures for assets and liabilities are listed. Income statement information is provided for three years, but without the helpful typical formatting for reading financial statements. Sixteen potential earnings per share (EPS) ratios are listed, such as EPS from continuing operations and diluted EPS from continuing operations. An indirect cash flow statement is presented along with ratio analysis for over thirty ratios. Quarterly information is also provided. Additionally, an extensive list of competitors, brands, major shareholders, top institutional stockholders, growth estimates, inside trading information, and analyst reports are presented.

> **EXAMPLE:** Pull up Barnes and Noble, find recent intellectual property, and determine whether the financial ratios in LexisNexis Academic consider its intellectual property assets.
>
> **Discussion:** Go to the company dossier, as shown in Figure 3.10, and enter "Barnes and Noble." The result shows a handful of companies. Select the public parent company headquartered in New York: Barnes and Noble, Inc. The search results then display the company snapshot. Select Intellectual Property Information on the left side of the snapshot screen. Note the categories for patents, trademarks, and copyrights divided by the United States, the European Union, and Japan. Selecting each patent item reveals no results for Barnes and Noble, unlike trademarks and copyrights.

Copyright 2011 LexisNexis, a division of Reed Elsevier Inc. All rights reserved. LexisNexis and the Knowledge Burst logo are registered trademarks of Reed Elsevier Properties Inc. and are used with the permission of LexisNexis.

The financial ratios from the detailed financial information do not consider the value of the intangibles. The references reveal that the company dossier has used a variety of notable sources for each category. For example, the competitive positioning part of the report is from Hoover's and the Directory of Corporate Affiliations.

Accounting information under the Subject Area folder in LexisNexis Academic is incomplete. LexisNexis Academic primarily provides nonauthoritative accounting sources. Furthermore, the database presents an alphabetical mismatch of sources from which to select, such as the AICPA's *Journal of Accountancy*, the SEC's financial reporting releases, and Wiley publications.

SUMMARY

The ability to do database research on a particular accounting issue, company, or business topic is an important skill for the twenty-first century. Extensive information on companies is available in commercial accounting, financial research, and literature search databases. The explosion of information has made it a necessity to understand popular databases. Many research tools are provided in databases to help the user conduct practical accounting research more effectively and efficiently. Many of the skills developed in using these databases can then be transferred to other databases used in practice.

The future financial accounting professional should practice using such databases as RIA Checkpoint, the SEC's EDGAR, S&P NetAdvantage, and LexisNexis Academic as well as other databases of value to accountants.

Knowledge Busters

This chapter provides a number of mini-cases called Knowledge Busters that will require you to conduct financial accounting research using the various databases discussed in Chapters 1–3 of this text, especially the FASB's Codification and eIFRS. The Knowledge Busters will help you not only to expand your financial accounting knowledge into some very specific accounting and technical issues, but also to become more familiar in navigating through the various databases that you will use as professional accountants. Completing these Knowledge Busters will provide valuable experience so you can complete the more challenging cases in Chapter 5.

Each Knowledge Buster will require you to reference specific sections of the authoritative literature in support of your recommended answer. Remember that, as you search the various databases, keywords or search phrases will aid you in identifying the specific sections of the authoritative literature that address the issue you are researching.

The following is a listing of the Knowledge Busters that are included in this chapter with the topic and the database(s) or website(s) to use in searching for answers to the specific questions raised.

Knowledge Buster	Topic	Database(s)
1	Location of Accounting Terms	FASB Codification
2	Codification Sections	FASB Codification
3	Revenue Recognition	FASB Codification
4	Repurchase of Loans	FASB Codification
5	Debt Classification	FASB Codification
6	Allowance Account	FASB Codification
7	Membership Dues	FASB Codification
8	Stock Dividends	FASB Codification
9	Inventory Valuation	FASB Codification
10	Barter Transactions	FASB Codification & eIFRS
11	Asset Retirement Obligations	FASB Codification & eIFRS
12	SEC Reporting Requirements	SEC Website
13	First-Time Adopters of IFRS	eIFRS
14	Location of Accounting Terms	eIFRS
15	Property, Plant, and Equipment	eIFRS
16	Segment Reporting	FASB Codification & eIFRS
17	Insurance Contracts	FASB Codification
18	Current Assets	FASB Codification
19	Interim Financial Statements	FASB Codification & eIRFS
20	Treasury Stock	FASB Codification

21	SEC Filings	SEC Website
22	Inventory	FASB Codification
23	Interest Capitalization	FASB Codification
24	Research and Development Costs	FASB Codification
25	Stock Subscription	FASB Codification

Knowledge Buster 1

Topic: Location of Accounting Terms
Database: FASB Codification

To gain familiarity with the content and organization of the FASB's Codification, you decide to test your knowledge/research skills by locating certain accounting terms. Utilizing the general topics presented below, determine where the following accounting terms would be located.

General Topic	Section
General Principles	100
Presentation	200
Assets	300
Liabilities	400
Equity	500
Revenue	600
Expenses	700
Broad Terms	800
Industry	900

Accounting Term	General Topic Section
Example: Receivables	300
Stock splits	____
Guarantees	____
Foreign currency matters	____
Start-up costs	____
Leases	____
Commitments	____
Principal agent/considerations	____
Derivatives and hedging	____
Real estate	____
Multi-element arrangements	____

Knowledge Buster 2

Topic: Codification Sections
Database: FASB Codification

To gain familiarity with the detailed section references (which include topic, subtopic, and section numbers) within the FASB's Codification, you decide to test your knowledge/research skills by locating the specific Codification references for the following issues.

Accounting Issue	Topic	Subtopic	Section
1. Gain contingencies disclosures			
2. Consolidation—recognition of research and development arrangements			
3. Treasury stock—initial measurement			
4. Inventory—subsequent measurement			
5. Investments—equity method and joint ventures—derecognition			
6. Cash and cash equivalents—SEC disclosure			
7. Advertising costs—recognition			
8. Financial instruments—registration payment arrangements—disclosure			
9. Income statement—extraordinary and unusual items—presentation matters			
10. Not-for-profit entities—split-interest arrangements—overview			

Knowledge Buster 3

Topic: Revenue Recognition
Database: FASB Codification

Medical Devices Inc. is a public company that trades its securities on the American Stock Exchange. Recently, its management, in reviewing year-end sales, has concluded that to meet budgeted sales numbers the company needs to increase sales in the month of December by $3 million. Management has determined that the company has products available to ship to customers prior to year-end. Medical Devices' CEO calls three specific customers and convinces each customer to order $1 million worth of products, which Medical Devices delivers prior to year-end.

In reviewing Medical Devices' normal and customary business practice for these types of customers, you notice that a written sales agreement with an authorized customer signature is required for the sale to be binding. Medical Devices prepared and signed the sales agreements and faxed them to the three customers prior to year-end. One customer signed and dated the agreement on 12/29 and returned it to Medical Devices. The other two customers did not sign their agreements until 1/10 of the following year due to a required review by their legal departments. However, they reported to Medical Devices that this was just a formality and the agreements should be returned by 1/15. As a result of these verbal commitments, the CEO had the accounting department record the $3 million as sales in the current year.

Required:

Medical Devices' controller is questioning whether the $3 million in sales related to these three customers can be recorded this year as revenue? Provide your response to the controller with appropriate citations from the FASB's Codification.

Knowledge Buster 4

Topic: Repurchase of Loans
Database: FASB Codification

Credit Financial often transfers its loans to other financial institutions with recourse in order to maintain a certain level of cash on hand. In the past, these transfers have been recorded as sales. However, Thrifty Cash is unable to collect on one of the loans bought from Credit Financial. Therefore, Credit Financial, under the recourse agreement, has agreed to reacquire the loan, and the purchase price of the loan is now greater than its fair value.

The controller of Credit Financial is somewhat uncertain as to how this repurchase should be recorded. He concludes that it seems logical to record the transaction at the purchase price rather than at fair value. His argument is that assets should be recorded at cost. To record the transaction as fair value would result in some type of loss, yet no sale of the repurchased loan has taken place!

The controller has requested your assistance to research the issue.

Required:

Utilize the FASB Codification to determine the proper treatment of the acquired loan where the purchase price is greater than the fair value.

> What keywords would you use in your search?
> What specific Codification references support your conclusion?

Knowledge Buster 5

Topic: Debt Classification
Database: FASB Codification

Jettison Manufacturing has been planning an expansion of its manufacturing facilities. As a result, in year 1, it obtained a $2 million long-term loan from National Bank. According to the debt agreement between the two parties, Jettison Manufacturing is required to maintain a current ratio of 2:1 or greater. At year-end, the controller concluded that the current ratio was only 1:1, and, therefore, Jettison was in violation of the debt agreement, requiring the loan to be paid to National Bank within six months.

Since Jettison was unable to obtain any concessions from National, Jettison reclassified the long-term debt as a current liability. However, within the first three months of the next year, Jettison has been able to correct the debt agreement violation and restore the current ratio to 2.2:1, which is acceptable to National. Therefore, the debt does not have to be repaid early.

In preparing year 2's financial statements, the controller is perplexed as to how to classify the debt—short term or long term? As controller, your assistance is necessary to settle the issue.

Required:

Utilize the FASB Codification to determine the proper classification of the debt.

What keywords would you use in your search?

What specific Codification references did you use in preparing your answer?

Knowledge Buster 6

Topic: Allowance Account
Database: FASB Codification

JIM: This year has been great for business with fantastic customers. This should definitely help our net income and bonuses for the year!

NANCY: Exactly what do you mean, Jim?

JIM: Well, with great customers who should pay their bills, we will not need to establish an allowance for doubtful accounts for our accounts receivable.

NANCY: Wait a minute, Jim. In my accounting classes, we always recorded bad debts expense and the related allowance account. Therefore, I believe we need to estimate our bad debts and prepare an adjusting entry at year-end.

JIM: But with good customers, I don't think it is required to establish an allowance account. Without recording bad debts expense, our net income should increase by $250,000, which definitely helps our year-end bonuses!

NANCY: We need to check whether this is acceptable under GAAP.

Required:

Use the FASB Codification to determine whether GAAP requires the establishment of an allowance account for all accounts receivable.

What keywords would you use in your search?

What specific Codification references support your conclusion?

Knowledge Buster 7

Topic: Membership Dues
Database: FASB Codification

Better Community, a new local not-for-profit entity, has been recently formed. The organizers of the entity have formalized operations in such a way that they will charge membership dues, but will not provide any specific services in exchange for the dues. In discussion with a local accountant, who is also a new member of the not-for-profit entity, the conclusion is reached that the dues will be recognized as contributions and recorded as revenue in the year received rather than over the period of membership.

In a review of the entity's operations, you find that additional services, such as seminars and group insurance, are provided by the entity. However, members are charged an additional cost for the aforementioned services. Because of this new information, you decide to investigate whether Better Community's recording of membership dues is appropriate.

Required:

Utilize the FASB's Codification to determine the appropriate accounting treatment for membership dues.

Knowledge Buster 8

Topic: Stock Dividends
Database: FASB Codification

Johnson Industries, which is having a very successful year, suggests to the Board of Directors that it issues a dividend to the stockholders. In the discussion with management, the members of the Board of Directors conclude that, in order to conserve cash for plant expansion, they will declare a 3% stock dividend in December of the current year to be distributed early next year.

As a result of this decision, the CFO of Johnson Industries, in preparing the financial statements, questions whether the stock dividend should be used in calculating the weighted average number of shares outstanding in the determination of earnings per share (EPS) for the current year, since the dividend will not be distributed until next year. The CFO turns to you for advice.

Required:

Determine the appropriate handling of the stock dividend in calculating EPS. Cite specific authoritative references to defend your answer.

Knowledge Buster 9

Topic: Inventory Valuation
Database: FASB Codification

National Drilling is a manufacturer of drill bits for large oil rigs that operate around the world. A major component in the manufacturing of the drill bits is diamonds. As a result of an increase in oil drilling due to the increase in oil prices, National Drilling has received, and is expected to receive, an increase in orders for new and replacement drill bits. With such a potential demand, National Drilling has purchased a large quantity of diamonds. Since diamonds are considered a precious metal, National Drilling is contemplating the proper valuation of its inventory, which currently is above cost.

Management has concluded that precious metals with a fixed monetary value and without substantial marketing costs can be recorded at market value, as discussed at a recent oil and gas conference that National's accounting staff attended. As a member of the staff, you question the proper valuation of the diamond inventory.

Required:

Utilizing the FASB's Codification, determine with specific authoritative reference the proper valuation of the diamond inventory.

Knowledge Buster 10

Topic: Barter Transactions
Databases: FASB Codification & eIFRS

JASON: I did not realize that our company enters into barter transactions.

JILL: I did not either. But I assume we remove the cost of the asset given up and replace it with the same value for the bartered item received.

JASON: I wonder though, since some of the barter transactions are with foreign entities, how these transactions would be recorded?

JILL: Well, it would depend if the companies are utilizing U.S. GAAP or IFRS.

JASON: Isn't the accounting the same under GAAP and IFRS?

JILL: Not necessarily.

JASON: We had better check as to the appropriate accounting if we ever decide to adopt IFRS.

Required:

Utilizing the FASB's Codification and eIFRS, prepare a report to Jason and Jill as to the appropriate accounting for barter transactions under U.S. GAAP and IFRS with specific references to the authoritative literature.

Knowledge Buster 11

Topic: Asset Retirement Obligations
Databases: FASB Codification & eIFRS

Zimmer Chemical Co. has chemical manufacturing facilities around the world. Recently, Zimmer erected a new facility in South Korea at a cost of $48 million and plans to operate the new facility for a period of fifteen years. The South Korean government requires that, at the time Zimmer concludes operations at the facility, Zimmer dismantle the facility and clean up any chemical spills that might have occurred at the location during manufacturing operations. The estimated cost of the dismantling and cleanup is $2 million.

Zimmer's management has concluded that the accounting for the asset retirement obligation (ARO) could be handled in one of three ways:

1. Record the $2 million as an expense at the time of dismantling and cleanup (at the end of the fifteen-year-life of the facility).
2. Increase the cost of the asset (manufacturing plant) by $2 million, for a total cost of $50 million.
3. Charge the $2 million to inventory, since the ARO should be part of production costs of inventory.

In discussions with the South Korean government, Zimmer is informed that the South Korean manufacturing facility will be required to prepare and report its financial statement in accordance with IFRS. As a result, Zimmer's managers are attempting to decide the acceptable accounting treatment for the ARO. They assume that the accounting is the same under U.S. GAAP and IFRS. They turn to you, the outside accounting firm representative, for advice.

Required:

Conduct research to determine the appropriate accounting recognition of the ARO under U.S. GAAP and IFRS. Prepare a report to be presented to Zimmer's management with specific authoritative literature references.

Knowledge Buster 12

Topic: SEC Reporting Requirements
Database: SEC Website

Clever Manufacturing Co., a public company that files various forms with the SEC, has recently been considered to be a very attractive growth stock and has been touted as a "buy" recommendation by various stock analysts. However, there have been recent disagreements among the members of its Board of Directors and between management and the independent auditors over various accounting issues. It seems that management over the last few years always adjusts the board's accounting estimates in a direction that increases income for the period. Two board members have disagreed with management's changing its estimates and have asked for advice from the independent accounting firm.

After some heated debates among the board, management, and the independent accounting firm, two board members have resigned from the board. After further discussion with the accounting firm, the accounting firm has decided to withdraw as independent auditors of Clever Manufacturing. The controller of Clever now informs management that, being a public company, Clever might need to inform the SEC of these changes on an SEC Form 8-K. Management disagrees and informs the controller to keep quiet as to these disagreements, as public disclosure could have a negative impact on the company's stock price.

The controller asks for your advice as to whether this type of inside discussion among the board, management, and independent accounting firm needs to be reported to the SEC.

Required:

Access the SEC's website, and, under rules and forms, determine whether the resignation of the two board members and the accounting firm needs to be disclosed to the SEC and, if so, when. (*Hint:* Search for Form 8-K requirements.)

Knowledge Buster 13

Topic: First-Time Adopters of IFRS
Database: eIFRS

Northwood Industries, a U.S.-based public company, has two subsidiaries located in Europe. These two subsidiaries are required to prepare their individual financial statements in accordance with IFRS. Northwood, contemplating that the SEC will soon requires U.S.-based public companies to file financial statements also in accordance with IFRS, has decided to check out the requirements.

The new controller at Northwood is seeking assistance as to whether any international standards address first-time adopters of IFRS and, more specifically, the requirements to the change to IFRS.

Required:

Utilize eIFRS to determine if there is an international standard applicable to first-time adopters. If so, what are the basic requirements for adoption of IFRS?

Knowledge Buster 14

Topic: Location of Accounting Terms
Database: eIFRS

To gain familiarity with the content and organization of eIFRS, you decide to test your knowledge of the location of certain accounting terms. Determine if any component of the IFRS (IFRSs, IFRICs, IASs, and SICs) applies to the following terms.

Accounting Term	IFRS
Construction contracts	_____
Financial instruments disclosures	_____
Share-based payment	_____
Employee benefits	_____
Interests in joint ventures	_____
Agriculture	_____
Earnings per share	_____
Borrowing costs	_____
Operating segments	_____
Accounting for government grants	_____

Knowledge Buster 15

Topic: Property, Plant, and Equipment
Database: eIFRS

JUSTIN: I always thought that property, plant, and equipment must be reported on a company's financial statements at cost.

MARY: I totally agree.

JUSTIN: Well, I noticed something strange in reviewing a foreign company's filing with the SEC.

MARY: Don't keep me in the dark! What was your great discovery?

JUSTIN: This foreign company, in its policies section footnote, stated that, after the initial recognition of property, plant, and equipment, the items are carried at a revalued amount.

MARY: That must be a mistake.

JUSTIN: Maybe IFRS allows such a revaluation.

MARY: Let's check it out.

Required:

Use eIFRS to determine if any international accounting standard focuses specifically on property, plant, and equipment (PP&E). Also, verify whether PP&E can be revalued subsequent to acquisition. Give specific references.

Knowledge Buster 16

Topic: Segment Reporting
Databases: FASB Codification & eIFRS

Many entities, especially large ones, offer a range of products and/or services to customers and often operate in several geographical locations. Since each product group or geographical area might be subject to differing rates of profitability, growth opportunities, and risks, the aggregated financial information provided in the entity's financial statements does not provide the details for segment analysis. Therefore, many entities are required to provide segment information to third parties. Specific questions often arising as to segment reporting are whether there are any quantitative thresholds for entities to follow and whether there is a difference between U.S. GAAP and IFRS requirements.

Required:

Utilizing the FASB's Codification and eIFRS, identify any differences that exist as to the quantitative threshold question. Provide specific authoritative references.

Knowledge Buster 17

Topic: Insurance Contracts
Database: FASB Codification

KYLE: I heard you recently left public accounting for a new job.
MATT: After 60- to 70-hour weeks, I decided to accept a fantastic offer from one of our clients.
KYLE: What company did you decide to go with?
MATT: American Insurance Company. I will be dealing with the accounting of insurance contracts.
KYLE: Sounds like a very technical area of accounting.
MATT: It sure is. I'm currently trying to learn the difference between cost recovery and the deposit method of accounting for various insurance contracts.

Required:

Provide specific Codification references that explain the two accounting models that Matt is investigating.

Knowledge Buster 18

Topic: Current Assets
Database: FASB Codification

MICHELLE: How did you do on that accounting exam?
NICOLE: I just missed a "B" by two points.
MICHELLE: At least you passed the exam!
NICOLE: I know. But I was hoping for a higher grade, since I studied so hard for this exam.

MICHELLE: Maybe there were some questions that the professor graded wrong.

NICOLE: I agree. We had one question that asked, "How should a deposit on a piece of equipment that is to be purchased within one year be classified on the entity's balance sheet?"

MICHELLE: That's easy. Even I know the answer to that question. It would be recorded as a current asset.

NICOLE: That's exactly how I answered the question, and it was graded wrong.

MICHELLE: You need to go to the professor and tell him that the grading guide is in error.

NICOLE: Before I do that, I want to be sure of the answer.

Required:

Utilize the FASB's Codification to provide a specific reference for Nicole on her issue.

Knowledge Buster 19

Topic: Interim Financial Statements
Databases: FASB Codification & eIFRS

EVAN: Jan, we have a new project to work on for next week.

JAN: What does it entail?

EVAN: Our project requires us to prepare not only annual financial statements, but also interim statements for quarterly reporting.

JAN: Does not appear to be too difficult. However, I think that the requirement for quarterly (interim) financial statements applies only to specific entities. Therefore, I don't believe we need to prepare them for our company.

EVAN: But the instructions indicate we need to prepare both annual and interim financial statements.

JAN: We had better check out the authoritative literature as to the requirements. Also, maybe for extra credit, let's check to see if IFRS has the same requirements as U.S. GAAP.

EVAN: Great idea!

JAN: Let's meet later today and plan our research attack.

Required:

Utilize the FASB's Codification and eIFRS to answer the following: (1) What entities have to prepare interim financial statements under GAAP? (2) Can annual costs (i.e., annual depreciation) be allocated to interim periods under U.S. GAAP and IFRS? Provide specific authoritative references.

Knowledge Buster 20

Topic: Treasury Stock
Database: FASB Codification

Nelson Industries, a U.S.-based company, has over the years issued 1 million shares of common stock to shareholders. Currently, in evaluating ownership, Nelson has entered into a stock repurchase agreement to buy a significant block of its stock from a major stockholder that represents a controlling interest in the company.

However, the major stockholder has agreed to sell at a price higher than the current market price. The stockholder has agreed to a price of $25 per share, which is in excess of the current market price of $20 per share.

Nelson's controller is somewhat unsure of the proper accounting for this purchase. She believes that the treasury stock purchase should be at the $20 per share price and the excess written off as some type of loss, since the purchase agreement does not include any other rights or privileges. The controller seeks your advice as to the proper accounting for the treasury stock repurchase.

Required:

Utilize the FASB's Codification to provide a recommendation to the controller for the treasury stock purchase transaction. Provide specific Codification references.

Knowledge Buster 21

Topic: SEC Filings
Database: SEC Website

The SEC requires companies to file various forms for specific financial reporting purposes. Below are listed various forms required to be filed with the SEC.

Required:

Utilize the SEC's website and describe what each form is used for.

Form	Description
Example: 10-K	Annual report pursuant to Sections 13 & 15(d) of the 1934 SEC Act
10-Q	_____
11-K	_____
18-K	_____
20-F	_____
40-F	_____
5	_____
8-K	_____
S-1	_____
6-K	_____
40-17F2	_____

Knowledge Buster 22

Topic: Inventory
Database: FASB Codification

Tires R Us is a wholesaling and retailing company that deals in automotive tires for foreign cars. During the year-end audit, heated discussion occurs between management and the independent auditors.

Management's accounting policy for valuing the inventory of imported tires reads as follows:

Inventory is valued at actual cost plus any freight-in. At year-end, the warehousing costs related to the tires are prorated to cost of goods sold and inventory on hand.

The auditors for Tires R Us believe that any warehousing costs should not be considered as inventory, but should be expensed as period costs. Management disagrees by stating that the warehousing costs would not have been incurred if the tires did not exist and therefore should be part of the value of inventory on hand. The CFO of the company has requested the auditors to justify their conclusion by providing specific authoritative support for their decision.

Required:

Utilize the FASB's Codification to provide a recommendation to the auditors to support their decision. Provide specific Codification references.

Knowledge Buster 23

Topic: Interest Capitalization
Database: FASB Codification

A&R Construction Company has been very successful over the past five years and now has decided that it needs to construct a building to house all of its equipment. The company's controller has notified management that any interest costs on funds obtained to construct the new building can be capitalized as part of the cost of the new building.

However, the vice president of finance has raised the following question for the controller: "I understand from your presentation that we can capitalize interest costs on the average amount of accumulated expenditures during the current year. But the building will not be completed until next year, and, therefore, do we capitalize only the interest costs on the average of current period expenditures?" The controller responded that the capitalization should be on the total expenditures. The vice president questioned again whether the controller is correct, since the expenditure made last year already included capitalized interest.

Required:

Utilize the FASB's Codification to write a report on the proper accounting for interest capitalization. Provide specific Codification references.

Knowledge Buster 24

Topic: Research and Development Costs
Database: FASB Codification

Scientific Laboratories, Inc. is contemplating a sale of the business to an unrelated third party. During the current year, Scientific has incurred substantial amounts of research and development (R&D) costs related to some drugs with a very high probability of future success.

Scientific's managers are negotiating the sale prior to the issuance of the current year's financial statements, and they have decided to capitalize the current year's R&D costs, since they are part of the negotiated selling price. The potential buyer however disagrees and informs Scientific that such R&D costs should not be capitalized.

Required:

Utilize the FASB's Codification to write a report on the proper accounting for R&D costs. Provide specific Codification references.

Knowledge Buster 25

Topic: Stock Subscription
Database: FASB Codification

Delfield Corporation has been contemplating the issuance of additional stock for funding a plant expansion, so it has entered into a stock subscription program that includes monthly payments for the purchase of its stock.

One potential subscriber enters into a stock purchase agreement with Delfield to buy 5,000 shares of Delfield's stock at a total price of $50,000 ($10/share), to be paid in four monthly payments of $12,500. The stock subscription agreement includes a statement that any payments made are nonrefundable. After two payments totaling $25,000, the subscriber defaults on the remaining two payments. As a result, Delfield has recorded the nonrefundable $25,000 paid as other income in the current financial statements.

Required:

Utilize the FASB's Codification to write a report on the proper accounting for the defaulted payments of $25,000. Provide specific Codification references.

Introduction to Research and Case Analysis

The first step in the research process is to read the case, understand the facts, and identify the problem or issue. Facts in short cases are usually rather clear. Real-life facts are often complex, however, even when simplified in cases. Thus, careful reading is a necessity.

The researcher must distinguish conclusions from underlying facts. Consider, for example, the statement that "the potential $500,000 liability from a lawsuit on patent rights was remote." "Remote" is a term of art in accounting requiring professional judgment before reaching that decision. Thus, the potential $500,000 liability from a lawsuit on patent rights is a fact. However, classifying the liability as remote is a conclusion.

In order to digest all of the facts, it often helps to diagram the parties or events. For any case analysis (be it a "real" case or a simplified case), one should routinely write one or two paragraphs on the facts before starting the research process. Failure to do so may waste valuable time.

The more familiar the researcher is with a client and its business, the better the researcher is able to interact with the client or its corporate management in order to ask insightful, pertinent questions to establish the facts. The researcher must use the client's time efficiently, but effectively. Thus, one may need to spend significant initial time with the client, but one should use discretion as to when to go back to the client for any additional facts needed.

After digesting the facts of a case, the researcher must critically identify the issue or issues for investigation. While knowledge of financial accounting terms is helpful in identifying the issues, the researcher should treat each case as if it is an accounting problem the researcher has never studied before. This approach will help ensure nothing is overlooked. Issue identification begins with selecting keywords from the facts or accounting literature, such as those in the glossary of the Codification. The researcher should write down the tentative issue(s) and plan to refine them as the research process progresses. The issue may expand from simple words to understanding the concept within the context of the critical facts. Therefore, as one refines the issue with greater sophistication, one will eventually have a statement that includes the critical facts, which may make a difference in the application of the authority. For example, a keyword from the previous example is the term "remote." Placing that term in the context of the facts helps to define the real issue (e.g., if a prior court decision on the term exists).

Research is exciting, but challenging. The foundation for mastering research was established in the first three chapters relating to databases. The researcher needs to decide what database and which part of the database to use to find the relevant information. Several areas of the database potentially addressing the problem should be examined, and persistence is often a required element of the research process.

Sometimes a clear answer to a research issue does not exist. Instead, one may need to exercise judgment based on the closest research on point. Thus, one applies a principal to an analogous situation. Remember to summarize the relevant research sources, along with their citations (their precise locations in the database) for easier return and client reference. Recall that IFRS is more principles-based than U.S. GAAP, often requiring additional documentation as to why an alternative was chosen.

As discussed in the opening chapters, keyword searches in a database are just one research method. Other methods, such as drilling down in a database or using an index to find the relevant topic, often work more effectively. These alternative approaches are especially used in the Codification and eIFRS. When one approach does not work effectively, alternative approaches should be considered until a viable solution is located. A difficulty with conducting research is deciding when to stop. Stopping may depend on the importance of the issue, time budget, relevant authority, amount at issue, and need to create a record of one's work on an issue. Sometimes it may seem like more than one alternative solution is possible. The researcher should record these alternatives and critically analyze them. Sometimes the research steps might lead to an iterative process. For example, through the current research process, the researcher might learn that certain facts are critical to deciding which part of the authority should be applied. Therefore, the researcher must double-check the facts of the case or refine the issue before reaching a conclusion based on reasoning.

Finally, the researcher must communicate the results. This communication depends on the researcher's situation. In class, the researcher might be expected to communicate a case brief comprising the issues, research sources, alternatives evaluated, and reasoned conclusion. Sometimes the researcher might be asked to present the case orally or to engage in a simulation involving role-play. All of these situations require advance preparation through reading the case multiple times to absorb the details.

In practice, writing a memo or letter in an email is very common. Sometimes an email delivers a short message on the conclusion, while the attached memo provides the facts, issue(s), research sources, alternatives examined, and reasoned conclusion. While the style is generally to the point because time is money, one needs to enable others to reach the same conclusion on the merits of the case.

By engaging in case studies, one develops the higher-order critical thinking skills necessary in a competitive global economy. Memorization and understanding of accounting principles are not enough to meet global standards for professional accounting practice. One must have the ability to interact well with clients in order to acquire all of the critical facts. One must have the intellectual ability to determine the issue(s). One must have an understanding of the databases to engage in effective and efficient research. Ingenuity and critical thinking skills are needed in developing and evaluating the alternatives. Communication skills enable one to convey the results with clarity and effectiveness.

PART A: HYPOTHETICAL CASE STUDIES

Case 1

Soroka Corporation: U.S. GAAP vs. IFRS: Intermediate I Case Study

Soroka Corporation (Soroka) distributes consumer electronics and computers throughout the United States. Its most recent unadjusted balance sheet appears in Table C1.1. Soroka values its inventory at the lower of cost or market (LCM), utilizing the last in, first out method (LIFO) The LIFO reserve on Soroka's December 31, 20X1, financial statements is $2,500,000. Soroka is organized and taxed as a Subchapter S corporation and has a December 31 year-end.

Due to increased market pressures and competition, Soroka is contemplating expanding into Canada, which already represents 25% of its customer base. The expansion would allow Soroka to reduce costs, resulting in a lower Canadian selling price. Ultimately, this should result in increased sales to existing customers and access to new customers. Canada currently reports under IFRS.

Soroka has hired you to recast its current balance sheet using IFRS. While working on this task, you find new items (not recorded in the financials unless stated) that need to be addressed under U.S. GAAP and IFRS:

- Soroka made a year-end inventory purchase with a cost of $165,000. Because the items were still in the shipping container, the internal accountant omitted the LCM valuation, although the receiving clerk appropriately included the purchase in the given balance sheet. Soroka intends to sell the inventory for $210,000. Estimated costs to dispose of the inventory are $30,000, and Soroka's normal profit margin is $20,000. Replacement cost is $155,000.
- Due to a recent real estate market decline, Soroka must evaluate its buildings for impairment. Buildings acquired for a cost of $460,000, with an associated accumulated depreciation of $92,000, have a fair value of $358,000. Selling costs are minimal. The undiscounted future value of expected cash flows from building use is $367,000. The discounted present value of expected cash flows is $359,000.
- With expansion talks in the news, customer relationships have increased in value to $292,000.
- Soroka has been working on creating a new handheld computer device to compete with the smartphone. Soroka spent $250,000 during the first quarter of 20X1 studying alternatives. During the second quarter of 20X1, Soroka spent an additional $25,000 improving one alternative to the point at which it became technologically and economically feasible. During the third quarter of 20X1, Soroka spent another $65,000 on the handheld computer to make it ready for use and sale by the end of the year.
- Included in Soroka's short-term debt is an $80,000 loan. Soroka refinanced it as long-term debt after year-end, but before the audited financial statements were issued.
- On November 10, 20X1, Customer A was shopping for a notebook computer in one of Soroka's stores. The screen cracked and severely cut Customer A's hands. Customer B (a child), running in the aisle, stepped on the glass. Both customers were brought to the hospital. Although there has been no litigation related to this event as of year-end, Soroka's legal counsel believes there is a 75% probability that Soroka will be sued by Customer A, resulting in a loss of between $200,000 and $300,000, with no estimate within the range being better than any other estimate. Legal counsel believes there is a 60% probability that Customer B will sue Soroka, resulting in a $50,000 loss.

Requirement A: Transaction Analysis under U.S. GAAP

1. List the authoritative guidance for each transaction.
2. Prepare journal entries for the transactions under U.S. GAAP. Be sure to show your calculations.
3. Prepare Soroka's closing balance sheet as of December 31, 20X1. Start with the unadjusted balance sheet and include any adjustments necessary to create the closing balance sheet.

Requirement B: Transaction Analysis under IFRS

4. Recast Soroka's December 31, 20X1, unadjusted balance sheet using IFRS.
5. List the authoritative guidance for each transaction.
6. Prepare journal entries for the transactions under IFRS. Be sure to show your calculations.

7. Prepare Soroka's closing statement of financial position as of December 31, 20X1. Start with the unadjusted statement of financial position and include any adjustments necessary to create the closing statement of financial position.

TABLE C1.1   Soroka's U.S. GAAP December 31, 20X1, Balance Sheet

Soroka Corporation
Balance Sheet
December 31, 20X1
Assets

Current Assets	
Cash and cash equivalents	$ 1,800,000
Accounts receivable (net of $30,000 allowance)	2,000,000
Inventory ($2,500,000 LIFO reserve)	5,400,000
Other current assets	1,150,000
Total current assets	10,350,000
Property, Plant, and Equipment	
Land	300,000
Capital lease equipment	100,000
Buildings	460,000
Fixtures and equipment	5,000,000
Accumulated depreciation	(3,400,000)
Net PPE	2,460,000
Goodwill	2,500,000
Intangible Assets	
Tradenames	160,000
Customer relationships (net of $10,000 amortization)	280,000
Total assets	$ 15,750,000

Liabilities and Shareholders' Equity

Current Liabilities	
Accounts payable	$ 5,300,000
Accrued liabilities	$ 1,700,000
Short-term debt	670,000
Current portion of long-term debt	35,000
Total current liabilities	7,705,000
Long-term debt	1,100,000
Long-term liabilities	605,000
Contingencies	50,000
Total liabilities	9,460,000
Shareholders' Equity	
Common stock	40,000
Additional paid-in capital	450,000
Retained earnings	5,800,000
Total shareholders' equity	6,290,000
Total liabilities and shareholders' equity	$ 15,750,000

Key Terms

Contingency	LIFO
Debt	Lower of cost or market
IFRS	Probable
Intangible assets	Property, plant, and equipment
Inventory	Refinance
Liability	Research and development

Readings:

Francesco Bellandi, "Dual Reporting under U.S. GAAP and IFRS," *The CPA Journal* 77, no. 12 (December 2007): 32–41

Hana Bohusova, "Revenue Recognition under US GAAP and IFRS Comparison," *The Business Review* 12, no. 2 (Summer 2009): 284–291.

Nadi Chan and Andrée Lavigne, "Seven Key Differences," *CA Magazine* 142, no. 5 (June–July 2009): 36–42.

Sylwia Gornik-Tomaszewski and Miguel A. Millan, "Accounting for Research and Development Costs: A Comparison of U.S. and International Standards," *Review of Business* 26, no. 2 (Spring 2005): 42–47.

Dahli Gray, "Accounting Profession Is Ready for International Financial Reporting Standards: Financial Statements Comparable Enough," *Journal of Applied Business Research* 26, no. 6 (November–December 2010): 27–32.

Peggy Ann Hughes, Nancy Stempin, and Matthew D. Mandelbaum, "The Elimination of LIFO: A Requirement for the Adoption of IFRS in the United States," *Review of Business Research* 9, no. 4 (2009): 148–155.

Richard C. Jones, "IFRS Adoption: Some General Issues to Remember," *The CPA Journal* 80, no. 7 (July 2010): 36–38.

Scott E. Miller, "Towards Convergence: A Survey of IFRS to U.S. GAAP Differences," *Journal of International Accounting Research* 8, no. 1 (2009): 70–71.

Source: Natalie T. Churyk, Northern Illinois University.

Case 2

Soroka Corporation: U.S. GAAP vs. IFRS: Intermediate II Case Study

Soroka Corporation (Soroka) distributes consumer electronics and computers throughout the United States. Its most recent unadjusted balance sheet appears in Table C2.1. Soroka values its inventory at the lower of cost or market, utilizing the last in, first out method (LIFO). The LIFO reserve on Soroka's December 31, 20X1, financial statements is $2,500,000. Soroka is organized and taxed as a Subchapter S corporation and has a December 31 year-end.

Due to increased market pressures and competition, Soroka is contemplating expanding into Canada, which already represents 25% of its customer base. The expansion would allow Soroka to reduce costs, resulting in a lower Canadian selling price. Ultimately, this should result in increased sales to existing customers and access to new customers. Canada currently reports under IFRS.

TABLE C2.1   Soroka's U.S. GAAP December 31, 20X1, Balance Sheet

Soroka Corporation
Balance Sheet
Assets December 31, 20X1
Assets

Current

Cash and cash equivalents	$ 1,800,000
Accounts receivable (net of $30,000 allowance)	2,000,000
Inventory ($2,500,000 LIFO reserve)	5,400,000
Other current assets	1,150,000
Total current assets	10,350,000

Property, Plant, and Equipment

Land	300,000
Capital lease equipment	100,000
Buildings	460,000
Fixtures and equipment	5,000,000
Accumulated depreciation	(3,400,000)
Net PPE	2,460,000
Goodwill	2,500,000

Intangible Assets

Tradenames	160,000
Customer relationships (net of $10,000 amortization)	280,000
Total assets	$ 15,750,000

Liabilities and Shareholders' Equity

Current Liabilities

Accounts payable	$ 5,300,000
Accrued liabilities	1,700,000
Short-term debt	670,000
Current portion of long-term debt	35,000
Total current liabilities	7,705,000
Long-term debt	1,100,000
Long-term liabilities	605,000
Contingencies	50,000
Total liabilities	9,460,000

Shareholders' Equity

Common stock	40,000
Additional paid-in capital	450,000
Retained earnings	5,800,000
Total shareholders' equity	6,290,000
Total liabilities and shareholders' equity	$ 15,750,000

Soroka has hired you to recast its current balance sheet using IFRS. While working on this task, you find new items (not recorded in the financials unless stated) that need to be addressed under U.S. GAAP and IFRS:

- On December 1, 20X1, Soroka invested $200,000 in shares of a closely held firm, Leah Enterprises (Leah), which it hopes to sell for a profit in the next few years.

Because Leah is not traded on an exchange, Soroka asked its valuation firm to determine Leah's year-end value. The valuation firm determined the investment is worth $198,000 at December 31, 20X1.

- On December 31, 20X1, Soroka issued $1,000,000 worth of 10-year, 6% convertible bonds at par. On the date of sale, the market rate of interest was 8%. Each $1,000 bond is convertible into 20 shares of common stock.
- Soroka leased equipment with the following terms. Soroka is required to pay the lessor $10,000 at the end of each year for the next seven years, at which time the equipment will have zero salvage value. Substantial modification costs will be involved to ready the equipment for another firm. Soroka's incremental borrowing rate is 6%. The implicit rate is unknown. The equipment has an economic life of ten years. Soroka's policy is to take a full year of depreciation in the year of acquisition for purchases and capital/finance leases. The title of the equipment remains with the lessor at the end of the lease, and there is no bargain purchase option. Both the cost and the fair value of the equipment are $62,200.
- Soroka issued $25,000 worth of redeemable preferred shares. The shares are redeemable if Soroka's 20X2 first-quarter net sales reach $2,500,000.
- During 20X1, Soroka adopted an employee defined-benefit pension plan. Soroka agreed to give employees credit for prior service in the amount of $35,000. The average remaining service equals the average remaining vested period of nonvested PSC, which equals 10 years. Fair value of plan assets on January 1, 20X1 = $0. Fair value of plan assets on December 31, 20X1 = $69,000. Projected benefit obligation (accumulated and present value) at January 1, 20X1 = $0. Projected benefit obligation (accumulated and present value) at December 31, 20X1 = $82,100. Actual return on plan assets = $4,000. Employer contributions during 20X1 = $65,000. Service cost for 20X1 = $45,000. Both the expected return and the discount rate equal 6%. Using only the information in this entry, account for the adopted plan. *Note:* Although many businesses no longer offer defined benefit plans, most, if not all, government agencies do.

Requirement A: Transaction Analysis under U.S. GAAP

1. List the authoritative guidance for each transaction.
2. Prepare journal entries for the transactions under U.S. GAAP. Be sure to show your calculations.
3. Prepare Soroka's closing balance sheet as of December 31, 20X1. Start with the unadjusted balance sheet and include any adjustments necessary to create the closing balance sheet.

Requirement B: Transaction Analysis under IFRS

4. Recast Soroka's December 31, 20X1, unadjusted balance sheet using IFRS.
5. List the authoritative guidance for each transaction.
6. Prepare journal entries for the transactions under IFRS. Be sure to show your calculations.
7. Prepare Soroka's closing statement of financial position as of December 31, 20X1. Start with the unadjusted statement of financial position and include any adjustments necessary to create the closing statement of financial position.

Key Terms

Bonds

Debt

Equity

Investments

Leases

Other comprehensive income

Other reserves

Pension

Preferred shares/stock

Redeemable

Shares

Readings:

Francesco Bellandi, "Dual Reporting under U.S. GAAP and IFRS," *The CPA Journal* 77, no. 12 (December 2007): 32–41.

Hana Bohusova, "Revenue Recognition under US GAAP and IFRS Comparison," *The Business Review* 12, no. 2 (Summer 2009): 284–291.

Nadi Chan and Andrée Lavigne, "Seven Key Differences," *CA Magazine* 142, no. 5 (June–July 2009): 36–42.

Dahli Gray, "Accounting Profession Is Ready for International Financial Reporting Standards: Financial Statements Comparable Enough," *Journal of Applied Business Research* 26, no. 6 (November–December 2010): 27–32.

Richard C. Jones, "IFRS Adoption: Some General Issues to Remember," *The CPA Journal* 80, no. 7 (July 2010): 36–38.

Scott E. Miller, "Towards Convergence: A Survey of IFRS to U.S. GAAP Differences," *Journal of International Accounting Research* 8, no. 1 (2009): 70–71

Source: Natalie T. Churyk, Northern Illinois University; modified from working paper with Alan Reinstein, Wayne State University, and Guy Gross, McGladrey.

Case 3

Supplyrite: Business Combination

Supplyrite distributes various small tools and supplies to industrial, commercial, institutional, and governmental markets throughout the United States. During the past two years, Supplyrite has seen a significant decrease in the demand for its products. As part of Supplyrite's long-term strategic plan, its management has been in negotiations to purchase 100% of Equipco in order to diversify Supplyrite's product offerings and customer base. Equipco distributes various-sized equipment to markets similar to Supplyrite's. Supplyrite and Equipco are both SEC registrants with June 30 year-ends. Ignore all tax effects.

At the close of business on June 30, 20X9, the two companies consummated their agreement whereby Supplyrite would purchase Equipco's common stock for $37,500,000 in cash and a $10,000,000 note payable to the sellers of Equipco.

The note payable to the sellers of Equipco carries an interest rate of 12% and will be paid off in equal quarterly principal installments of $500,000.

In order to finance this transaction, Supplyrite, as the borrower, obtained a $37,500,000 note payable from a financial institution, which is to be repaid in equal monthly installments over ten years, plus interest at 9%.

Equipco values its inventory utilizing the last in, first out method (LIFO). The LIFO reserve on Equipco's June 30, 20X9, financial statements is $2,500,000.

Supplyrite engaged an appraiser to determine the fair value of Equipco's fixed assets as of June 30, 20X9. Equipco's fixed assets have been appraised as follows:

- Land $ 1,250,000
- Buildings $ 3,475,000
- Transportation equipment $ 750,000
- Computer equipment $ 675,000
- Furniture and fixtures $ 55,000

Supplyrite has also engaged a valuation firm to assist it in identifying and valuing any intangible assets that exist as part of this transaction as of June 30, 20X9. The intangible assets identified are as follows:

- Customer relationships $ 8,675,000
- Tradename $ 2,325,000
- Noncompete agreement $ 1,295,000

Supplyrite incurred various transaction costs as part of the acquisition of Equipco. Those costs comprise the following:

- Accounting fees $ 325,000
- Legal fees $ 575,000

Equipco also incurred various transaction costs relating to its sale. Those costs comprise the following:

- Accounting fees $ 80,000
- Broker fees $ 2,475,000
- Legal fees $ 215,000

The fair market value of all other assets and liabilities not identified above is assumed to be the same as their current carrying value as of June 30, 20X9.

Equipco's June 30, 20X9, balance sheet appears in Table C3.1.

Requirement A: Business Combination Accounting under U.S. GAAP

1. List the authoritative guidance under U.S. GAAP for this transaction.
2. Compute the purchase price of this transaction.
3. Prepare Equipco's opening balance sheet as of July 1, 20X9, starting with the June 30, 20X9, closing balance sheet and including any adjustments necessary.

Requirement B: Business Combination Accounting under IFRS

4. Reformat Equipco's June 30, 20X9, balance sheet into an IFRS statement of financial position.
5. List the authoritative guidance under IFRS for this transaction.
6. Compute the purchase price of this transaction.
7. Prepare Equipco's opening statement of financial position as of July 1, 20X9, starting with the June 30, 20X9, closing statement of financial position from requirement 4. Include necessary adjustments. *Note:* For case study purposes, prepare the statement of financial position using the required method under U.S. GAAP.

Key Terms

Business combination   Intangible assets
Fair value   Transaction costs
Goodwill

Readings:

Seán Callaghan and Marie Treacy, "Business Combinations: How Recent Changes to FASB and IASB Standards Will Impact Your Business," *Accountancy Ireland* 40, no. 4 (August 2008): 14–17.

Kang Cheng and Sharon G. Finney, "It's Coming: M&As under IFRS," *The Journal of Corporate Accounting and Finance* 21, no. 3 (March–April 2010): 13–18.

TABLE C3.1   Equipco's U.S. GAAP June 30, 20X9, Balance Sheet

Equipco
U.S. GAAP
Balance Sheet
June 30, 20X9
Assets

Current Assets

Cash	$ 35,500
Accounts receivable, less allowance for doubtful accounts of $85,000	17,000,000
Inventory, less allowance for obsolescence of $250,000	19,000,000
Prepaid expenses	189,500
Total current assets	36,225,000

Property and Equipment

Land	500,000
Buildings	2,250,000
Transportation equipment	900,000
Computer equipment	535,000
Furniture and fixtures	150,000
	4,335,000
Less accumulated depreciation	3,100,000
	1,235,000
Goodwill	8,000,000
Other assets	350,000
Total assets	$ 45,810,000

Liabilities and Stockholders' Equity

Current Liabilities

Note payable, bank	$ 4,000,000
Accounts payable	10,390,000
Accrued expenses	3,710,000
Total current liabilities	18,100,000
Deferred Compensation	5,600,000
Stockholders' Equity	
Common stock	10,000
Additional paid in capital	13,000,000
Retained earnings	9,100,000
Total stockholders' equity	22,110,000
Total liabilities and stockholders' equity	$ 45,810,000

James W. Deitrick, "What Analysts Should Know about FAS No. 141R and FAS No. 160," *Financial Analysts Journal* 66, no. 3 (May–June 2010): 38–44.

Hugo Nurnberg, "Certain Unresolved Ambiguities in Pushdown Accounting," *The CPA Journal* 80, no. 9 (September 2010): 14–16, 18–21.

P. J. Patel, "Current Issues in Accounting for Business Combinations," *Financial Executive* 26, no. 5 (June 2010): 57–59.

Peter Woodlock and Gang Peng, "How Will Valuation Changes Affect M&A Deals?" *The Journal of Corporate Accounting and Finance* 20, no. 4 (May–June 2009): 49–61.

Source: In-class case: Natalie T. Churyk, Northern Illinois University; Guy M. Gross, Partner, McGladrey; and Robert Stoettner, Partner, McGladrey; modified for working paper with Alan Reinstein, Wayne State University.

Case 4

Mesa Building Products: Impairment

Background

Mesa Building Products (Mesa) distributes various building products to new home builders throughout the United States. Mesa has begun to see a decrease in the building of new homes. As part of Mesa's long-term strategic plan, Mesa's management negotiated to purchase La Paz Home Renovations (La Paz) in order to diversify Mesa's product offerings and customer base. La Paz provides home renovation services as well as distributing various building products used in the home renovation industry. Mesa and La Paz are both organized and taxed as Subchapter S corporations and have December 31 year-ends.

At the close of business on December 31, 20X6, the two companies consummated their agreement whereby Mesa would purchase La Paz's common stock for $40,000,000 in cash and a $10,000,000 note payable to the sellers of La Paz.

Mesa engaged an appraiser to determine the fair value of La Paz's fixed assets and intangibles other than goodwill as of December 31, 20X6. La Paz's books reflect those values.

The note payable to the sellers of La Paz carries an interest rate of 12% and will be paid off in equal quarterly principal installments of $500,000, beginning March 31, 20X7.

In order to finance this transaction, Mesa, as the borrower, obtained a $40,000,000 note payable from a financial institution, which is to be repaid in equal monthly installments over ten years, plus interest at 9%, beginning January 31, 20X7.

Current Situation

During 20X8, Mesa and La Paz have continued to see a downturn in both new housing starts and the home renovation industry. During the audit planning meeting with Mesa's external auditors, the carrying value of La Paz's intangibles was discussed.

To address the Mesa auditors' concerns regarding potential impairment, Mesa has engaged a valuation firm to assist it in determining, at December 31, 20X8, the fair value of both La Paz and La Paz's current intangibles.

The valuation firm's report detailed out the following fair values as of December 31, 20X8:

- Fair value of La Paz $ 30,000,000
- Customer relationships $ 7,500,000
- Tradename $ 3,000,000
- Noncompete agreement $ 250,000

Mesa also asked the appraisal firm that performed the original fixed asset appraisals to perform an update of its work. The appraised values of the fixed assets as of December 31, 20X8, were determined to be as follows:

- Land $ 1,100,000
- Buildings $ 3,400,000
- Transportation equipment $ 775,000
- Computer equipment $ 100,000
- Furniture and fixtures $ 125,000

As a result of these appraisals, it was determined that the appraised values above exceeded their current net book values as of December 31, 20X8.

Mesa's management has determined that La Paz is a separate and stand-alone reporting unit, and Mesa's external auditors have concurred with that assessment.

Assume that all other assets and liabilities not discussed above have carrying values that equal fair value at December 31, 20X8.

La Paz's December 31, 20X8, balance sheet and statement of financial position before considering the above valuation are attached as Table C4.1 and Table C4.2 of this case.

Requirement A: Impairment Analysis under U.S. GAAP

1. List the authoritative U.S. GAAP guidance that needs to be followed to address the auditors' concerns regarding the potential impairment of certain asset classes held by La Paz.
2. Prepare a U.S. GAAP impairment analysis of La Paz's intangible assets as of December 31, 20X8.
3. Prepare La Paz's balance sheet as of December 31, 20X8, including any adjustments necessary based on the valuation and appraisal discussed above. Show the unadjusted December 31, 20X8, balance sheet, along with a column and detail of all adjustments deemed necessary, which cross-foots to the final adjusted December 31, 20X8, balance sheet.

Requirement B: Impairment Analysis under IFRS

4. List the authoritative IFRS guidance that needs to be followed to address the auditors' concerns regarding the potential impairment of certain asset classes held by La Paz.
5. Prepare an IFRS impairment analysis of La Paz's intangible assets as of December 31, 20X8.
6. Prepare La Paz's statement of financial position as of December 31, 20X8, including any adjustments necessary based on the valuation and appraisal discussed above. Show the unadjusted December 31, 20X8, statement of financial position, along with a column and detail of all adjustments deemed necessary, which cross-foots to the final adjusted December 31, 20X8, statement of financial position.

Key Terms

Fair value	Impairment
Goodwill	Intangible assets

Readings

Eugene E. Comiskey and Charles W. Mulford, "Goodwill, Triggering Events, and Impairment Accounting," *Managerial Finance* 36, no. 9 (2010): 746–767.

Michael J. Mard, James R. Hitchner, and Steven D. Hyden, *Valuation for Financial Reporting: Fair Value Measurements and Reporting, Intangible Assets, Goodwill and Impairment*, 2nd ed. (Hoboken, NJ: John Wiley & Sons, Inc., 2007).

Source: In-class case: Natalie T. Churyk, Northern Illinois University; Guy M. Gross, Partner, McGladrey; and Robert Stoettner, Partner, McGladrey; modified for working paper with Alan Reinstein, Wayne State University.

TABLE C4.1   La Paz U.S. GAAP December 31, 20X8, Balance Sheet

La Paz Home Renovations
Balance Sheet
December 31, 20X8
Assets

Current Assets	
Cash	$ 75,000
Accounts receivable	12,000,000
Inventory	16,000,000
Prepaid expenses	100,000
Total current assets	28,175,000
Property and Equipment	
Land	1,000,000
Buildings and improvements	3,500,000
Transportation equipment	885,000
Computer equipment	125,000
Furniture and fixtures	175,000
	5,685,000
Less accumulated depreciation	950,000
	4,735,000
Goodwill	18,040,000
Intangible Assets	
Customer relationships, net of accumulated amortization of $2,125,000	6,375,000
Tradename, net of accumulated amortization of $500,000	2,000,000
Noncompete agreements, net of accumulated amortization of $500,000	750,000
	9,125,000
Other assets	350,000
Total assets	$ 60,425,000

Liabilities and Stockholders' Equity

Current Liabilities	
Note payable, bank	$ 8,000,000
Note payable, former shareholder, La Paz	2,000,000
Accounts payable	3,000,000
Accrued expenses	2,375,000
Total current liabilities	15,375,000
Long-Term Liabilities	
Note payable, former shareholder, La Paz	4,000,000
Deferred compensation	5,200,000
Total long-term liabilities	9,200,000
Stockholders' Equity	
Common stock	10,000
Additional paid-in capital	41,340,000
Retained earnings	(5,500,000)
	35,850,000
Total liabilities and stockholders' equity	$ 60,425,000

TABLE C4.2   La Paz IFRS December 31, 20X8, Statement of Financial Position

La Paz Home Renovations
Statement of Financial Position
December 31, 20X8

	Dec 31, 20X8 Unadjusted Balance
Noncurrent assets	
Property, plant, and equipment	
Land	$ 1,000,000
Buildings and improvements	3,500,000
Transportation equipment	885,000
Computer equipment	125,000
Furniture and fixtures	175,000
	5,685,000
Less accumulated depreciation	950,000
	4,735,000
Goodwill	18,040,000
Intangible assets	
Customer relationships, net of accumulated amortization of $2,175,000	6,375,000
Tradename, net of accumulated amortization of $400,000	2,000,000
Noncompete agreements, net of accumulated amortization of $600,000	750,000
	9,125,000
Other noncurrent assets	350,000
Total noncurrent assets	32,250,000
Current assets	
Cash	75,000
Accounts receivable	12,000,000
Inventory	16,000,000
Prepaid expenses	100,000
Total current assets	28,175,000
Total assets	**$ 60,425,000**
Current liabilities	
Note payable, bank	8,000,000
Note payable, former shareholder, La Paz	2,000,000
Accounts payable	3,000,000
Accrued expenses	2,375,000
Total current liabilities	15,375,000
Noncurrent liabilities	
Note payable, former shareholder, La Paz	4,000,000
Deferred compensation	5,200,000
	9,200,000
Total liabilities	**$ 24,575,000**
Net assets	**$ 35,850,000**
Stockholders' equity	
Share capital	$ 10,000
Share premium	$ 41,340,000
Retained earnings	(5,500,000)
Total stockholders' equity	$ 35,850,000

PART B: REAL-LIFE CASE STUDIES

Case 5

Diebold: Revenue Recognition, Leases, Capitalization, and Inventory

Selected excerpts from Diebold's public records are the basis for this case. Diebold is an Ohio-based company that manufactures and sells automated teller machines (ATMs), bank security systems, and electronic voting machines.

In 20X4, Diebold had a standard form contract for customer purchases. The form converted orders for which Diebold recognized revenue upon installation at the customer site to "bill and hold" transactions. Thus, the contract contained a boilerplate clause stating that the customer had requested Diebold to hold items for the customer's convenience. Diebold then recognized revenue when the company shipped the products from its factory to its warehouse using the "ship to warehouse" date contained in the contract rather than the date when the purchase was installed.

For example, in the fourth quarter of 20X4, at the direction of company management, a Diebold sales representative had Customer A sign a bill and hold form to convert a $4 million order to a purported bill and hold transaction. On a conference call, the sales representative advised company management that Customer A had signed the bill and hold form. That form, by its terms, required payment upon receipt of the invoice when Diebold shipped the products to its warehouse. However, in reality by side agreement, Customer A would not pay for the ATMs before installation. Company management nevertheless recognized revenue on the transaction.

Diebold recognized revenue on this transaction in the fourth quarter of 20X4. Even though Customer A was invoiced in the fourth quarter of 20X4, it did not pay for this transaction until the second quarter of 20X5 (after Diebold had delivered and installed the products). This transaction increased Diebold's earnings in the fourth quarter of 20X4 by approximately $2 million. By prematurely including the revenue from the Customer A transaction, Diebold was able to report that it met the low end of the quarter's projected earnings. Without the revenue from the Customer A transaction, Diebold would have missed its projected earnings.

Diebold management encouraged its sales force to "make the quarter." Calls requested that customers execute the bill and hold forms despite concerns raised by sales personnel. For example, in June 20X5, a Diebold sales manager wrote an email to Diebold management stating that the sales staff was "trying to help Diebold's revenue recognition drive," but also raising concerns about asking customers to sign bill and hold forms if Diebold was at fault for installation delays. The email was forwarded to an officer of the company, who took no action at the time to correct this practice. Another employee responded to the sales manager's original email stating: "This is like the crazy aunt in the cellar no one wants to talk about."

Diebold's $7.5 Million Revenue Recognition Reserve

In January 20X4, as part of its 20X3 year-end audit, Diebold's auditor tested a sample of Diebold's 20X3 bill and hold transactions. This testing found that Diebold had recognized revenue on certain transactions and that in certain instances Diebold had recognized revenue on transactions in a manner inconsistent with company policy. In response, Diebold established a $7.5 million reserve (based on the 20X3 fourth-quarter profit margin) by extrapolating the errors found in the auditor's sample.

In February 20X4, management learned that Diebold had prematurely recognized revenue in the fourth quarter of 20X3 on a $5.2 million order from Customer B. Because the company's auditor did not discover the error during its testing, Diebold management did not correct it. Additionally, Diebold did not adjust its $7.5 million profit margin reserve that it had established to account for auditor-detected errors.

Diebold's Failure to Disclose Its Revenue Recognition Practices

Prior to 20X4, Diebold did not disclose to shareholders that it had any bill and hold transactions, even though purported bill and hold transactions constituted a material portion of Diebold's revenues. Diebold management became concerned that the company's revenue recognition practices would not withstand scrutiny. Thus, in 20X4, Diebold made changes to its revenue recognition practices. Although these changes did not eliminate Diebold's use of bill and hold accounting, they did reduce the number of such transactions.

The Impact of Diebold's Revenue Recognition Practices

In the first quarter of 20X5, Diebold entered into an agreement to lease ATMs located in Company C stores to a private company, Cash Depot, for $5 million. In this transaction, Diebold entered into a side buy-back agreement with Cash Depot, giving Cash Depot the right to sell the ATMs back to Diebold at a later date. Diebold recognized all $5 million in revenue on this transaction in the first quarter of 20X5, which accounted for approximately 8% of Diebold's total pretax earnings that quarter.

Release of the $7.5 Million Revenue Recognition Reserve

As previously mentioned, Diebold established a $7.5 million reserve in the last quarter of 20X3. Over the course of 20X4, Diebold management released the reserve, without any accounting analysis. Diebold released $1 million of the reserve in the first quarter of 20X4, $1.25 million in the second quarter of 20X4, and the remaining $5.25 million in the third quarter of 20X4. Diebold exactly met the analyst earnings consensus for the first two quarters and met the revised analyst earnings consensus in the third quarter.

Under-Accrued Liabilities

Diebold increased earnings by failing to accrue for known liabilities. For example, the company's Long-Term Incentive Plan (LTIP) was an employee benefit plan intended to reward long-term company performance. Diebold management knew that the liability account for the LTIP was under-accrued for much of 20X2 and 20X3. In a May 9, 20X3, email from one officer to another, the officer explained U.S. GAAP as applied to the LTIP. At the time of this email, the officer's calculations indicated that the LTIP was under-accrued by at least $5 million.

To accrue for the LTIP in 20X3 without negatively impacting earnings, Diebold offset the liability by reducing other accounts, including an unreconciled accounts payable account and an unreconciled deferred revenue account. Indeed, Diebold management made one such $1.2 million offsetting journal entry in May 20X3. The description in the notes to that journal entry was "to fund a LTIP reserve." In 20X3 alone, Diebold management's manipulation of these accounts had the effect of under-accruing Diebold's liabilities and overstating Diebold's reported pretax earnings by at least $16 million.

Manipulating Other Reserves

From 20X2 to 20X6, Diebold management manipulated certain reserves in order to manage earnings. For example, to meet internal forecasts, a Diebold accounting manager reduced a liability account established for payment of customer rebates to inflate net income in both the fourth quarter of 20X3 and the fourth quarter of 20X4. Diebold knew, or was reckless in not knowing, that there was no legitimate accounting basis for either of these entries. Indeed, both entries were subsequently reversed in later quarters.

Delaying and Capitalizing Inventory

The value of a finished goods inventory account from 20X3 through 20X5 was overstated. Nevertheless, Diebold did not reconcile the account until 20X5. Then Diebold spread $15 million worth of expenses over two quarters. The overstatements increased Diebold's earnings by $4.3 million in 20X3 and more than $6.2 million in periods prior to 20X3.

The Oracle Project

In 20X2, Diebold began a project, which is still ongoing, to replace many of its older internal software systems with Oracle software. From 20X3 through 20X6, Diebold capitalized information technology costs. Diebold management also made top-level entries to capitalize additional expenditures to the Oracle project. These "additions" often were round numbers such as $1 million. Diebold's capitalization enabled it to reduce pretax earnings in 20X3, 20X4, and 20X5 by $.5 million, $3 million, and $6.8 million, respectively.

Used Equipment Write-Ups

From 20X3 to 20X5, Diebold management "wrote up" the value of certain used inventory, such as used ATMs. These write-ups had the effect of reducing the cost of goods sold and were used to meet forecasts.

For example, in the second quarter of 20X4, Diebold wrote up the value of its used equipment inventory by $1 million (and thus increased net income by $1 million) to help earnings meet forecasts. An accounting manager wrote in a July 13, 20X4, email: "I followed up with [a company officer] this morning. The primary reason we needed to book the used equipment-valuation was due to the overall corporate tax rate being a little higher than that which was forecasted. The tax rate change resulted in an approximate $500K problem in Net Income. As a result, we need a little more NIBT [net income before taxes] to deliver the required Net Income."

In another example, in the fourth quarter of 20X3, Diebold wrote up the value of parts contained in some used ATMs by $650,000. Tellingly, these parts were never removed from the ATMs, and the ATMs were later scrapped. Furthermore, Diebold wrote up the value of other used equipment inventory by $750,000 in the fourth quarter of 20X4 and $1.2 million in the first quarter of 20X5.

Requirement A: Reserve Accounts

1. Answer the following, including the U.S. GAAP authority in your answer.

    a. Who must request that a transaction be on a bill and hold basis?
    b. What accounting or disclosure is required for long-term incentive plans?
    c. How does an issuer account for anticipated liabilities?
    d. How should a company value its used equipment inventory?
    e. How are software development costs treated?
    f. When is a liability released?
    g. What is the treatment for maintaining general or excess reserves?
    h. How are material errors treated?

2. Which of Diebold's transactions were improper under GAAP?

3. What SEC authority was published in December 20X3 that, among other things, reiterated the criteria for bill and hold accounting?

Requirement B: Strategic Considerations

4. As a result of Diebold's accounting practices from at least 20X2 to 20X7, what would you expect the company to do?
5. If given the choice between maintaining books under U.S. GAAP and IFRS, are there strategic advantages for Diebold to switch to IFRS?

Readings

Robert M. Bowen, Angela K. Davis, and Shivaram Rajgopal, "Determinants of Revenue-Reporting Practices for Internet Firms," *Contemporary Accounting Research* 19, no. 4 (Winter 2002): 523.

Mustafa Ciftci, "Accounting Choice and Earnings Quality: The Case of Software Development," *European Accounting Review* 19, no. 3 (2010): 429.

Lori Olsen and Thomas R Weirich, "New Revenue-Recognition Model," *The Journal of Corporate Accounting and Finance* 22, no. 1 (November–December 2010): 55.

Josef Rashty and John O'Shaughnessy, "Revenue Recognition for Cloud-Based Computing Arrangements," *The CPA Journal* 80, no. 11 (November 2010): 32.

Sources: SEC, Accounting and Auditing Enforcement Release No. 3137, June 2, 2010.
SEC v. Diebold, Inc., Civil Action No. 1:10-CV-00908 (D.D.C. June 2010). (This case uses substantial excerpts from this public record.)

Case 6

Dell: Reserves and Disclosure of Vendor Payments

Substantial excerpts from the Dell Inc. (Dell) public record are the basis for this case. Dell is a Fortune 100 company and a key player in the personal computer market. Because Michael Dell founded the company in his University of Texas dorm room, the company was loved by investors, analysts, and business journalists.

Dell worked hard in order to meet analysts' quarterly earnings projections. It achieved this from 20X1 until 20X7 by using two tactics: reserve accounts and pressure on a major vendor, Intel, to make extra payments to Dell.

Reserve Accounts

"Cookie jar" reserves and other special reserve accounts were used to manage Dell's financial results. These cookie jar reserves consisted of excess, unsupported balances that resided in accounts controlled by the corporate finance group. For fiscal years 20X2 to 20X5, Dell created and maintained excess accruals in multiple reserve accounts to offset the financial statement impact of future expenses.

The reserves misstated Dell's operating expenses (OpEx) as a percentage of revenue (OpEx ratio), resulting in misstated quarterly trends in this ratio from about the second quarter of 20X0 through about second quarter of 20X5. The OpEx ratio was an important financial metric that the company itself highlighted. Each decrease in the ratio was described as achieving a "record low." Each instance where the ratio remained flat was portrayed as maintaining the "record low." Dell attributed achieving or continuing the "record lows" to "cost reduction initiatives" or a "focus on cost controls."

From 20X2 to 20X5, Dell maintained several accrued liability accounts. One account was a general reserve Strategic Fund, a cookie jar reserve. Dell referred to this fund as "corporate contingencies." Dell used the corporate contingencies primarily to reduce its future OpEx by releasing these excess accruals when unforecasted expenses arose. Dell executives frequently referred to another accrued liability account by its number, 24990.

Dell tracked the corporate contingencies in schedules entitled "Estimated Contingencies in Corporate" (hereinafter corporate contingency schedules). Dell's chief accounting officer (CAO) asked his subordinates to provide him those schedules at least once per quarter. The CAO directed subordinates to transfer "excess" accruals (previously reserved amounts no longer needed for bona fide liabilities) to the corporate contingencies. In the fourteen quarters from the first quarter of 20X2 through the second quarter of 20X5, Dell made at least twenty-three releases from the Strategic Fund and other corporate contingencies, sixteen of which were recorded after quarters ended, while Dell was in the process of closing its books.

Pressure on the Vendor

Intel made exclusivity payments to Dell in order for Dell not to use central processing units (CPUs) manufactured by its rival—Advance Micro Devices, Inc. (AMD). Without the Intel payments, Dell would have missed the earnings per share (EPS) consensus in every quarter. In the twenty quarters from the first quarter of 20X2 through the fourth quarter of 20X6, Dell met analysts' EPS consensus in fifteen quarters and exceeded consensus by 1 cent in five quarters.

The CAO noted that Dell's reliance on Intel payments was a strategic "problem." He stated that for three quarters now, Intel money had made the quarter and that this was a bad way to run the railroad. The payments made it appear that Dell was consistently meeting Wall Street earnings targets and reducing its operating expenses through the company's management and operations.

These exclusivity payments grew from 10% of Dell's operating income in 20X3 to 38% in 20X6 and peaked at 76% in the first quarter of 20X7. Dell failed to disclose the basis for the company's sharp drop in its operating results in the second quarter of 20X7 when Intel dramatically cut its payments after Dell announced its intention to begin using AMD CPUs. In dollar terms, the reduction in Intel exclusivity payments was equivalent to 75% of the decline in Dell's operating income.

From the first quarter of 20X7 to the second quarter of 20X7, Intel's extra payments fell by $263 million. Prior to this point, there had been only one quarter in the history of Intel's program during which the rebates had not increased the quarter after AMD filed its private antitrust lawsuit. In the first quarter of 20X7, Dell's reported operating income was $949 million. In the second quarter, Dell's operating income declined to $605 million.

Dell told investors that the sharp drop in the company's operating results was attributable to Dell pricing too aggressively in the face of slowing demand and to component costs declining less than expected. Yet Michael Dell, as CEO and the CFO, reviewed, approved, and signed Dell's annual reports on Forms 10-K and 10-Q and signed the Sarbanes–Oxley certifications.

Dell would often seek additional rebates from Intel in order to close a gap between its forecasted results and its earnings targets. Dell was quite open with Intel about the reasons it was requesting additional money.

Despite the "material" impact that Intel's extra payments had on Dell's operating results, Dell did not disclose any information relating to the payments in any of its annual or quarterly reports filed with the SEC for the periods from the first quarter of 20X3 through the first quarter of 20X7.

Many of Dell's materially misleading statements and omissions were made in the Management Discussion and Analysis of Financial Condition and Results of Operations (MD&A) section of Dell's Forms 10-K and 10-Q filed with the SEC during the relevant period. This section of Dell's financial reports is important to Dell's investors because it provides investors an opportunity to look at the company through the eyes of management.

Schnieder, the CFO, was a Certified Public Accountant (CPA) and a former audit partner with Price Waterhouse. Nonetheless, Schneider signed one or more management representation letters to PricewaterhouseCoopers (PwC) in which he certified that Dell's consolidated financial statements complied with U.S. GAAP even though he knew, or was reckless in not knowing, that Dell's accounting for the corporate contingencies was not in conformance with GAAP. Schneider also reviewed, approved, signed, and/or certified the accuracy of Forms 10-K and 10-Q that materially misstated Dell's financial results because of Dell's improper accounting for the corporate contingencies.

Dell received substantial assistance in connection with the corporate contingencies from Jackson, the corporate controller. Jackson received several emails with the corporate contingency schedules attached. These schedules tracked excess reserves, and Jackson often communicated with others about the corporate contingencies. Copies of the schedules were kept in a quarterly closing binder that Jackson maintained and used when briefing top finance executives. A CPA and former senior accountant at Arthur Young and Ernst & Young, Jackson signed one or more management representation letters to PwC in which she certified that Dell's consolidated financial statements complied with GAAP. Jackson also reviewed the Forms 10-K and 10-Q.

Requirement A: Reserve Accounts and Disclosure Practices

1. Did Dell violate U.S. GAAP? If so, what part of GAAP did Dell fail to follow?
2. Were the disclosures sufficient for the reserve accounts?
3. Did Dell have a duty under GAAP to disclose Intel's extra payments?
4. If Dell has a duty to disclose Intel's payments, what should be included in the disclosure?

Requirement B: Strategic Considerations

5. How might the reserves impact employees?
6. Do the problems at Dell require any other type of disclosure?
7. What do you expect Dell to have filed with the SEC? When is a restatement required under U.S. GAAP?
8. If Dell had the option to switch to IFRS, would Dell have had fewer problems? Explain.

Readings

Marsha B. Keune and Karla M. Johnstone, "Disclosures: Descriptive Evidence from the Revelation of Accounting Misstatements," *Accounting Horizons* 23, no. 1 (March 2009): 19.

Gary McWilliams, "Leading the News: Dell's Earnings Rose 31% in Quarter—Shipments Surged by 29% as Focus on Small Business and Consumers Paid Off," *Wall Street Journal*, May 16, 2003, Eastern edition, A.3.

Andy Serwer, "Dell's Midlife Crisis," *Fortune* 152, no. 11 (November 28, 2005): 147.

Xue Wang, "Increased Disclosure Requirements and Corporate Governance Decisions: Evidence from Chief Financial Officers in the Pre- and Post-Sarbanes-Oxley Periods," *Journal of Accounting Research* 48, no. 4 (September 2010): 885.

Sources: SEC, Accounting and Auditing Enforcement Release No. 3156, July 22, 2010.
Securities and Exchange Commission v. Dell Inc., Civil Action No. 1:10-CV-01245 (D.D.C. July 2010). (This case uses substantial excerpts from this public record.)

Case 7

E*TRADE

A. Introduction to Securitizations and Deferred Taxes

The following case reprints substantial parts of *E*TRADE v. Deutsche Bank AG*, 631 F. Supp. 2d 313 (S.D.N.Y. 2009), but shortens and simplifies the case for the reader interested in the accounting aspects of the case. The lengthy decision in the legal case was written by the Honorable Robert W. Sweet, U.S. District Judge. This case is divided into three parts: the introduction, the servicing fees, and the effective tax rates.

E*TRADE seeks to recover damages for breach of contract and fraud, as well as prejudgment interest, costs, and attorneys' fees, from defendant Deutsche Bank AG arising from the sale of two Deutsche Bank subsidiaries, Ganis Credit Corporation (Ganis") and Deutsche Recreational Asset Funding Corporation (DRAFCO) to E*TRADE, pursuant to a stock purchase agreement (the SPA) agreed to by the parties on November 25, 20X2.

The Parties and Related Entities

Plaintiff E*TRADE is a Delaware corporation with its principal place of business in New York, New York. The company provides online consumer financial services including securities trading, banking services, and loans.

Defendant Deutsche Bank is a German corporation with its principal place of business in Frankfurt, Germany. Its stock is traded on the New York Stock Exchange. At all relevant times, it had approximately 300–400 subsidiaries in the United States.

Ganis was a wholly-owned subsidiary of Deutsche Bank. Ganis originated and serviced consumer loans on recreational vehicles (the loans). DRAFCO, a subsidiary of Ganis, securitized and serviced recreational end-user financing loans originated by Ganis. DRAFCO had no employees, and the DRAFCO balance sheet contained only assets and liabilities related to securitizations of the loans originated by Ganis.

The Securitizations

Securitizations are complicated transactions. They involve specialized aspects of tax accounting because of the many cash flows and multiple parties (trusts, borrowers, investors, and companies selling the loans). They require substantial amounts of backup and legal documentation. DRAFCO completed four securitizations before its sale to E*TRADE, three in 20X0 and one in 20X1 (the securitizations). Each securitization had the same structure and involved several parties: borrowers, Ganis, DRAFCO, a trust, and investors.

The accounting for each securitization enabled Deutsche Bank to record a large book gain on the day the securitization closed and defer the taxes it had to pay on that gain. Securitization accounting "inflates income and reduces taxes immediately payable."

Ganis provided loans to the borrowers, who took on an obligation to make monthly payments of principal and interest to Ganis. A portion of this interest payment was allocated to pay for the cost of servicing the loans. Ganis transferred the loans to DRAFCO so that DRAFCO could *securitize* them while Ganis *serviced* them. After receiving the loans from Ganis, DRAFCO sold them to a trust.

The investors purchased notes that promised them a specified rate of interest. When the borrowers made their principal and interest payments on the Ganis loans, the trust used the proceeds to make payments to the investors. The residual interest reflected on the DRAFCO books was an estimate of the present value of future cash flows that DRAFCO would receive from the "excess interest" generated by each securitization. Excess interest is the difference between (1) the interest rate paid by the borrowers on the loans and (2) the interest rate paid to holders of the notes plus expenses associated with the loans. The interest rate paid on the loans was intended to generate enough cash to more than cover the interest paid on the notes plus expenses.

The residual interest from the securitizations appeared on E*TRADE's books beginning October 20, 20X3, the date E*TRADE purchased DRAFCO as set forth below. The residual interest from the 20X1 securitization is the only residual interest that currently remains on E*TRADE's books.

As previously stated, Ganis serviced the loans underlying each securitization. Servicing a loan portfolio involves providing services such as collecting and applying the monthly payments from the borrowers, maintaining records, sending out statements, making collection calls, and initiating foreclosure proceedings as necessary. Ganis performed such services for many financial institutions. For this service, Ganis was entitled to receive servicing fees, calculated as a percentage of the amount of the loans, as compensation. From 20X0 through 20X2, Ganis received $28 million in servicing fees directly from each trust on DRAFCO's behalf. In securitizations, the accounting for income and expenses is different for financial reporting purposes (book purposes) than for tax reporting purposes (tax purposes). For book purposes, U.S. GAAP governs the reporting of income and expenses. Under U.S. GAAP, securitizations are considered to be a sale, meaning the loans in question here were treated as if DRAFCO had sold them to the trusts. Thus, the loans were removed from DRAFCO's books the day each securitization closed. Also on the day each securitization closed, DRAFCO recorded for book purposes all income and expenses (including servicing fees) associated with it. The difference between the resulting entry (the residual interest) and the up-front cash received is the gain on sale (i.e., the estimated net profit from the securitization). DRAFCO did not record for book purposes any income or expenses after the date of securitization.

Deferred Taxes

A temporary deferred tax asset (DTA) resulted from the accounting treatment of the securitizations because, during the course of the securitization, there was a difference between when the taxpayer recorded the income and/or expense and when the amount of each item of income and expense "turned" (i.e., was the same for both tax purposes and book purposes).

For book purposes, all income and expenses related to each securitization were recorded on the day the securitization closed, and no income and expenses were recorded over the life of the securitization. For tax purposes, no income and expenses were recorded on the day each securitization closed, and all income and expenses were recorded as realized over the life of the securitization.

Requirement A:

1. Where in U.S. GAAP is the authority for accounting for securitizations?
2. What disclosures must be made with respect to securitizations?
3. What is a temporary difference? A permanent difference? Which gives rise to deferred taxes?
4. How does GAAP define deferred taxes? What authority governs the definition?
5. Describe the types of deferred taxes (e.g., deferred tax asset).
6. Where in GAAP is the authority for the calculation of deferred taxes?
7. Does a deferred tax arise from a securitization? If so, how do you calculate the deferred tax from a securitization? Provide the authority along with each answer.
8. What are the advantages of securitizing loans?

B. The Servicing Fees

Each month over the life of the securitization, DRAFCO recorded for tax purposes the income from the loans and related expenses. For book purposes, DRAFCO did not record any income or expenses, since they were recorded when the securitization closed. Taxable income ultimately exceeded book income, creating a DTA.

According to E*TRADE, the servicing fees should have been deducted as incurred over the life of the securitization for tax purposes. The fees were included in the calculation of the residual interest for book purposes. Deutsche Bank's failure to deduct the servicing fees on DRAFCO's tax returns gave rise to the major dispute in this case.

The pro forma federal tax returns of DRAFCO and the calculations of its DTA (or DTL) were prepared in St. Louis by Deutsche employee Terry Hickam (Hickam). Hickam was not a securitization expert, and she relied on their auditor, KPMG, to create a Microsoft Excel template to calculate the value of DRAFCO's DTA. Hickam was responsible for inserting dollar amounts from the cash flows related to the securitizations into the template to calculate the DTA.

A note contained in the template stated: "Since interest income and expense is reported gross, it is not necessary to include servicing fee income. If the net spread is the starting point for M-1, service fee income will need to be added back." Hickam read this as an instruction to not deduct the servicing fee expenses paid by DRAFCO in the monthly calculation of the DTA. Hickam followed the KPMG template mechanically. The template monitored all of the temporary differences related to the gain on sale from the securitizations and multiplied them by an effective tax rate.

The Stock Purchase Agreement

For strategic reasons, Deutsche Bank decided in 20X0 to sell its "non-core businesses." E*TRADE typically insisted on audited closing balance sheets when it purchased a business. Consistent with this practice, E*TRADE requested that Deutsche Bank provide E*TRADE with independently audited closing balance sheets for DRAFCO and Ganis as a condition of closing.

The parties signed the SPA on November 25, 20X2. Article II of the SPA covered the purchase and sale of Ganis and DRAFCO. Pursuant to SPA § 2.02, the purchase price for the shares of Ganis and DRAFCO was to be the "tangible stockholders' equity" of those companies, plus a premium based on the value of Ganis's receivables.

Tangible stockholders' equity was to be determined by the total stockholder equity listed on the Ganis reference balance sheet used for the sale (adjusted for certain technical matters) less the value of its goodwill and the items listed in the "DRAFCO" column of the reference balance sheet.

In SPA § 3.06, Deutsche Bank represented that the reference balance sheet "present [ed] fairly in all material respects the financial condition and results of operations of the Business" and was "in accordance with U.S. GAAP."

By April 20X3, KPMG was in the process of auditing DRAFCO's residual. KPMG determined that Deutsche Bank's valuation of the residual was too high and refused to sign off on the value of the residual. Because the residual was an estimate of future cash flows associated with the previously described loans, its valuation was based on numerous assumptions about the loans' future performance. Actual losses on the loans were higher than anticipated due to a greater than expected number of borrowers defaulting.

KPMG told Deutsche Bank that "a lot of work has to be done" for KPMG to examine Deutsche Bank's assumptions and complete the audit of the residual. Any changes to these assumptions would cause the value of the residual to change. By mid-June 20X3, Deutsche Bank had revised the value of the residual downward. Yet it had not convinced KPMG to sign off on Deutsche Bank's revised valuation.

As a matter of accounting, the $23.3 million write-down of the residual (from $73.2 million listed on the reference balance sheet down to $49.9 million) increased the value of the DTA by approximately $9 million. This increase stemmed from the temporary difference resulting from the way a write-down is recorded for book and tax purposes. Accounting rules allowed DRAFCO to take the $23 million book deduction immediately, while tax rules did not allow DRAFCO to take the deduction immediately.

This $9 million increase in the DTA was added to the approximately $6 million DTA listed on the reference balance sheet, which resulted in a $15 million DTA. The audited closing balance sheet then represented that DRAFCO had three assets totaling approximately $65 million: a $25 million residual, $25 million in cash, and a $15 million DTA.

The audited closing balance sheet included KPMG's Independent Auditors' Report (Audit Opinion). Among other things, the Audit Opinion certified that (a) KPMG "conducted [its] audit in accordance with auditing standards generally accepted in the United States of America" (U.S. GAAS) and (b) the audited closing balance sheet "presents fairly, in all material respects, the financial position of [DRAFCO] as of December 23, 20X2, in conformity with U.S. GAAP". Note 5 to the audited closing balance sheet addressed income taxes and certified that the value of the DTA was $15 million.

E*TRADE first learned of the $15 million valuation of the DTA on July 18, 20X3, when it received the audited closing balance sheet from Deutsche Bank. Prior to this, E*TRADE knew only of a $6 million DTA represented on the reference balance sheet. Belinda Montgomery relied on KPMG's Audit Opinion and believed the $15 million DTA was accurate. She recommended to her superiors that E*TRADE should purchase the DTA. When E*TRADE received the audited closing balance sheet, no one at E*TRADE believed that it did not present fairly the financial condition of DRAFCO or that it violated U.S. GAAP.

Deutsche Bank used the template to create the spreadsheet it sent E*TRADE on August 21, 20X3. The spreadsheet listed fourteen temporary differences. Because Deutsche Bank employees understood the template instructions as directing them not to deduct servicing fee expenses, a temporary difference for servicing fee expenses was not contained on the spreadsheets.

When E*TRADE signed the purchase agreement on October 20, 20X3, it was unaware of any issue involving the DTA arising out of the failure to deduct the servicing fees. Montgomery relied on KPMG's Audit Opinion and believed the $15 million DTA was accurate. She would not have recommended to her superiors that E*TRADE purchase DRAFCO if she had known or suspected that the audited closing balance sheet was inaccurate. Based on her recommendation, E*TRADE's management team decided to purchase DRAFCO, including the DTA.

The Dispute Following the DRAFCO Closing

In November 20X3, as part of E*TRADE's regular year-end preparation of its financial statements, E*TRADE began conducting its annual review of the DTA. This also included having E*TRADE's auditor, Deloitte, audit E*TRADE's financial statements. The audit included its tax provisions, pursuant to SEC rules.

In its review of the DTA, Deloitte came to believe that the DTA on the audited closing balance sheet was substantially overstated because Deutsche Bank failed to deduct from its tax returns the approximately $28 million in servicing fee expenses that DRAFCO incurred. This would result in a reduction in the value of the DTA by approximately $11 million.

On November 21, 20X3, Deloitte had a telephone conference with Montgomery and others at E*TRADE. During the call, Deloitte informed E*TRADE for the first time that it appeared that Deutsche Bank had failed to deduct the servicing fee expenses and that, if this was true, the DTA would be significantly overstated. The E*TRADE employees reacted with shock and surprise.

For book purposes, the securitizations had been characterized as a sale. DRAFCO deducted all of the servicing fee expenses on the day each securitization closed because this expense reduced the value of the residual—"the traditional practice." On February 6, 20X4, Deutsche Bank stated that, while it failed to deduct the servicing fee expenses, this expense was a "permanent difference" that had no effect on the DTA.

In September 20X4, Deloitte refused to issue an independent audit opinion certifying the value of the DTA because E*TRADE could not substantiate it. Deloitte would not approve E*TRADE's financial statements if these statements included the DTA.

E*TRADE needed an independent audit opinion certifying its financials. E*TRADE ultimately determined that it should write off the entire DTA with the offset to goodwill because, while the parties "had roughly nine months of calls, exchanges, email exchanges of information," Deutsche Bank had failed to justify the $15 million valuation. Effective September 30, 20X4, E*TRADE wrote off the $15 million DTA.

KPMG admitted to E*TRADE that its work papers "were a mess" and that they could not reconstruct the audit. KPMG testified that much of the information needed to conduct this analysis was not contained in the work papers. KPMG's inability to reconstruct the DTA through its own work papers indicated to E*TRADE that the details used to support the original DRAFCO Audit Opinion either never existed or were improperly stated and kept.

KPMG internally and informally recognized that the DTA was overstated due to the failure to take the servicing fee deduction, but was institutionally committed to not changing its Audit Opinion. Deutsche Bank was a substantial client paying KPMG fees of approximately $50–$60 million annually.

Conclusion

The template, as utilized by Deutsche Bank, failed to deduct $28 million in servicing fees that DRAFCO had paid Ganis to service the loans. The failure to deduct these servicing fees inflated the amount of temporary differences used to calculate the DTA by $28 million, which, in turn, overstated the value of the DTA on the closing balance sheet by about $11 million, after multiplying by the effective tax rate.

The $28 million in servicing fees that Deutsche Bank incurred were legitimate business expenses of DRAFCO. DRAFCO's pro forma tax returns prior to 20X3 should have reflected a deduction of the servicing fees. The nature of the servicing fees that Deutsche Bank deducted in 20X3 was identical to that of the servicing fees Deutsche Bank did not deduct between 20X0 and 20X2. Thus, there was no reason to treat the servicing fees any differently.

The servicing fee expenses were accounted for when incurred for book purposes. They were recorded in the residual and used in the gain on sale calculations. The notes to DRAFCO's audited closing balance sheet (drafted by Deutsche Bank) stated: "The calculation of a gain or loss upon the sale of receivables in a securitization includes an estimation of the fair value of residual interest cash flows from receivables after the payment of interest and principal to investors and the servicing fee."

Requirement B:

9. Did Deutsche Bank violate U.S. GAAP? If so, explain how. Give the authority.
10. Give the GAAP authority for the proper treatment of servicing fees.
11. What strategic events were made regarding the servicing fees?
12. What accounting mistakes were made by each of the firms and characters?

C. The Effective Tax Rate

The spreadsheet sent to Montgomery on September 11, 20X3, used a 35% federal tax rate and a 7% state tax rate, which led to a blended tax rate of 39.55%. State tax is deductible on federal tax returns, and this deduction then reduces the blended tax rate from 42% (the sum of the state and federal tax rates) to 39.55%.

Montgomery was told that DRAFCO had filed a state tax return because DRAFCO was included in Deutsche Bank's California Unitary Tax Return. Montgomery concluded that DRAFCO had paid California state income tax and that it was appropriate for Deutsche Bank to use a 7% state tax rate because "the corporate tax rate in California is 8.84 percent."

The Audit Opinion, which KPMG represented as being prepared in accordance with U.S. GAAP, certified that the 39.55% rate complied with U.S. GAAP and was the proper tax rate for calculating the DTA. In the note to the Audit Opinion entitled "Income Taxes," KPMG wrote, "DRAFCO files individual or combined state income tax returns in accordance with state tax laws."

The Audit Opinion led Montgomery to believe that DRAFCO had paid state taxes, and E*TRADE relied on the Audit Opinion in agreeing to purchase the DTA. However, Deutsche Bank had "never paid state taxes" in any state, including California. While DRAFCO was part of Deutsche Bank's consolidated California tax return, it did not pay any income tax to the State of California. Deutsche Bank did not advise E*TRADE that "DRAFCO has never paid state taxes and, therefore, any DTA should be calculated at the 35% federal rate."

The federal tax rules allow a company to deduct the amount of state tax paid from federal taxable income. DRAFCO's 20X2 pro forma federal tax return deducted $1.6 million in state taxes that it had allegedly paid, and the 20X1 return deducted $71,053 in state taxes. Deutsche Bank was not entitled to take, and should not have taken, these deductions for state tax paid because DRAFCO failed to pay any state tax in 20X1 and 20X2.

Based on the state tax deductions in the 20X1 and 20X2 returns, E*TRADE reasonably believed, prior to the DRAFCO closing, that DRAFCO paid more than $1.6 million in state income taxes in 20X1 and 20X2. These returns supported E*TRADE's belief that it was proper for Deutsche Bank to use the 39.55% blended rate (which took into account a 7% state tax rate) to calculate the DTA.

KPMG stated in a note in its work papers: "Unsure at this time what states the company is subject to tax in." Deutsche Bank had not shown how it arrived at the 7% rate (as opposed to any other rate).

Damages

E*TRADE's direct damages are $11 million, the overstated amount of the DTA. First, E*TRADE has shown the impact of not considering the servicing fee expenses and liquidation expenses. The damage to E*TRADE caused by Deutsche Bank's failure to take these tax deductions was foreseeable. E*TRADE is entitled to recover for Deutsche Bank's failure to take these deductions (tax consequences are an element of damages when they are reasonably foreseeable and flow from the breach of contract). Second, E*TRADE has applied the correct tax rate of 35%.

	As Presented to E*TRADE ($ millions)	Actual ($ millions)
1. 14 listed temporary differences	$39	$39
2. Servicing expenses		($28)
3. Total temporary differences	$39	$11
4. Applicable tax rate	39.55%	35%
5. Deferred tax asset (Line 4 multiplied by Line 5)	$15	$4
DAMAGES	$11	

However, as shown on the previous page, E*TRADE paid $15 million (measured as of December 20X2) for an asset worth approximately $4 million. The purchase price did not accurately reflect the value of the purchased asset, and E*TRADE is entitled to recover the difference between the amount it paid for the asset and the actual value of the asset.

Requirement C:

13. Precisely where in U.S. GAAP is the authority for the effective tax rate for deferred taxes?
14. How did U.S. GAAP prohibit Deutsche Bank from using a state tax rate to calculate the DTA?
15. Strategically, explain the benefit of purchasing a deferred tax asset.
16. If a contract is made before the United States adopts IFRS as new U.S. GAAP, what do you suggest is needed in the contract between E*TRADE and Deutsche Bank?

Readings:

Gregory S. Miller and Douglas J. Skinner, "Determinants of the Valuation Allowance for Deferred Tax Assets under SFAS No. 109," *The Accounting Review* 73, no. 2 (April 1998): 213.

Elizabeth O'Brien, "Target: RIAs: E*Trade Seeks a Greater Foothold in the Crowded Wealth Management Arena," *Financial Planning*, September 1, 2006, 1.

Brett Philbin and John Kell, "E*Trade's Loss Widens," *Wall Street Journal*, April 29, 2009, Eastern edition, C.5.

Sources: *E∗TRADE Fin. Corp. v. Deutsche Bank AG*, 631 F. Supp. 2d 313 (S.D.N.Y. 2009). *E∗Trade Fin. Corp. v. Deutsche Bank AG*, 582 F. Supp. 2d 528 (S.D.N.Y. 2008).

Case 8

Lehman

A. Repo 105 Theory

This case is an abbreviated version of Bankruptcy Examiner Anton R. Valukas's report on Lehman Brothers and its discussion of Repo 105 transactions. That report was filed in bankruptcy court.

In late 20X1 and 20X2, Lehman employed off-balance-sheet devices known within Lehman as Repo 105 transactions. Such transactions temporarily removed securities inventory from its balance sheet. The removal typically lasted for a period of seven to ten days. Repo 105 transactions were nearly identical to standard repurchase and resale (repo) transactions that Lehman (and other investment banks) used to secure short-term financing. The critical difference was that Lehman accounted for Repo 105 transactions as sales rather than financing transactions. The rationalization for this was based on the overcollateralization or higher than normal "haircut" in a Repo 105 transaction. Simply put, the Repo 105 rationalization transformed a normal financing transaction into an asset disposal.

In a typical repo, a financial institution borrows funds using securities (usually treasuries) as collateral. For example, if a bank has securities (bonds) valued at $105, it will borrow $100 from another institution and present the securities as a guarantee for the short-term loan. The $5 difference is called a haircut and is the price for both the liquidity of the bond and its risk. It is important to note that repo markets are not new— they were born at the beginning of the twentieth century—and they have served a very legitimate purpose.

Like other large investment banks, Lehman engaged daily in tens of billions of dollars of ordinary repo transactions in its normal course of business. The ordinary repo transactions that Lehman conducted were treated as financing transactions. The transferred securities inventory remained on Lehman's balance sheet during the term of the repo, and the incoming borrowed cash increased Lehman's total assets. Total liabilities also increased because Lehman recorded a corresponding liability representing its obligation to repay the borrowed cash.

While simplified and for illustrative purposes only, the five illustrations that follow demonstrate the impact of an ordinary repo transaction and a Repo 105 transaction on Lehman's balance sheet and leverage ratios.

Lehman reported in its Forms 10-Q and 10-K that it treated repo transactions as financing transactions for accounting and reporting purposes.

Illustration 1: Simplified Balance Sheet

Assume this simplified balance sheet for Lehman:

Assets (in millions)		Liabilities	
Cash	$ 7,500	Short-term borrowings	$ 200,000
Financial instruments	350,000	Collateralized financings	325,000
Collateralized agreements	350,000	Long-term borrowings	150,000
Receivables	20,000	Payables	98,000
Other	72,500	Stockholders' equity	27,000
Total	$ 800,000		$ 800,000

The ratios calculated for comparison of the five illustrations are as follows: Gross leverage is total assets divided by stockholders' equity. Net leverage equals total assets minus collateralized agreements divided by stockholders' equity. For Illustration 1, gross leverage = 30; net leverage = 17.

Illustration 2: Modification of Illustration 1 Using a Typical Repo

Illustration 2 shows the impact of an ordinary repo on Lehman's balance sheet and leverage ratios. If Lehman executes $50 billion worth of typical repo transactions with $50 billion of its financial instruments, three consequences arise: (1) Those instruments remain on Lehman's balance sheet; (2) Lehman receives a $50 billion cash borrowing, increasing its cash position; and (3) Lehman records $50 billion worth of additional collateralized financing liabilities. At the moment of the repo transactions, the total balance sheet and leverage increase, as shown:

Assets (in millions)		Liabilities	
Cash	$ 57,500	Short-term borrowings	$ 200,000
Financial instruments	350,000	Collateralized financings	375,000
Collateralized agreements	350,000	Long-term borrowings	150,000
Receivables	20,000	Payables	98,000
Other	72,500	Stockholders' equity	27,000
Total	$850,000		$850,000

The ratios now increase as follows: gross leverage = 31; net leverage = 19.

Illustration 3: Modification of Illustration 2 by Paying Down Liabilities

Illustration 3 shows the impact of an ordinary repo followed by the use of the borrowed cash to pay down liabilities. Assuming Lehman uses the $50 billion cash borrowing from typical repo transactions to pay off current liabilities, the effect on the balance sheet is neutral—no net increase in total assets/liabilities and no effect on leverage:

Assets (in millions)		Liabilities	
Cash	$ 7,500	Short-term borrowings	$ 200,000
Financial instruments	350,000	Collateralized financings	**325,000**
Collateralized agreements	350,000	Long-term borrowings	150,000
Receivables	20,000	Payables	98,000
Other	72,500	Stockholders' equity	27,000
Total	**$800,000**		**$800,000**

The ratios now equal those in the simplified case, Illustration 1: gross leverage = 30; net leverage = 17.

Lehman publicly reported that it treated all repo transactions as financing transactions for accounting purposes. Yet in many instances Lehman booked Repo 105 transactions as sales. Superseded U.S. GAAP provided that those in the very large markets for repurchase agreements are mostly unaccustomed to treating those transactions as sales. "[A] change to sale treatment would have a substantial impact on their reported financial position."

The recasting of a repo transaction from a financing or "borrowing" transaction to a "sale" transaction leads to several major consequences: The transferred securities inventory is derecognized; it is considered sold and removed from the transferor's/seller's balance sheet during the term of the repo. This happens even though the transferor/seller is required to repurchase the inventory at a future date. Additionally, when a repo transaction is characterized as a sale, the transferor/seller does not record a liability representing its obligation to repay the borrowed funds. In other words, the "borrowing" is not reflected on the balance sheet, even though the economic substance of the transaction is a borrowing, and, thus, the transferor's total liabilities do not increase.

Although the transferor's inventory decreases, *at the moment* of the transaction the transferor's total assets remain unchanged because the transferor receives cash borrowings in exchange for the securities inventory. Consequently, Lehman's Repo 105 transactions removed securities inventory from Lehman's balance sheet for the duration of the repo—typically, seven to ten days.

At the moment of the Repo 105 transaction, Lehman received cash. By the nature of the "sale," inventory was reduced on the balance sheet, and the corresponding incoming cash was recorded. There was no overall effect on the gross assets, as one asset replaced another. By recording the Repo 105 transactions as sales, rather than as financings, Lehman was not required to record any liabilities arising from the obligation to repay the short-term funding secured by the Repo 105 transactions. Consequently, as demonstrated in Illustration 4 below, Lehman was able to borrow tens of billions of dollars without disclosing the borrowing.

Illustration 4: Repo 105

If Lehman executes $50 billion worth of Repo 105 transactions, rather than typical repos, the three major consequences are (1) the transactions are characterized as sales, and

$50 billion worth of financial instruments are considered sold and removed from the balance sheet; (2) Lehman receives $50 billion in cash, exchanging one form of asset for another and leaving total assets unchanged; and (3) Lehman records no corresponding liability for repayment of cash because there is no "obligation" to return the cash. Similar to gross assets, liabilities remain unchanged.

Assets (in millions)		Liabilities	
Cash	$ **57,500**	Short-term borrowings	$ 200,000
Financial instruments	**300,000**	Collateralized financings	325,000
Collateralized agreements	350,000	Long-term borrowings	150,000
Receivables	20,000	Payables	98,000
Other	72,500	Stockholders' equity	27,000
Total	**$800,000**		**$ 800,000**

It is important to note that the excess of inventory carrying value over cash received—the nominal 5% spread—was reported as a forward purchase derivative asset. In order to simplify the case at hand and isolate the "sale" versus "financing" issue, Illustrations 3 and 4 do *not* include the $5 derivative.

Lehman used the borrowed funds from Repo 105 transactions to pay down short-term liabilities such as repo borrowings, as shown in Illustration 5. Lehman could state a net leverage of 18.0x instead of 16.3x without Repo 105, which indicates that Lehman used Repo 105 cash to pay down different liabilities.

Given that Lehman undertook $39 billion, $49 billion, and $50 billion of Repo 105 transactions at quarter-end in the fourth quarter of 20X1, first quarter of 20X2, and second quarter of 20X2, respectively, Lehman's disclosures of its cash holdings at each quarter-end further strengthen the testimony and other evidence that Lehman used the cash borrowing from Repo 105 transactions to pay down short-term liabilities. *See* LBHI 20X1 Form 10-K, on p. 86 (reporting that Lehman had $7.286 billion in cash and cash equivalents on November 30, 20X1). While Lehman's Repo 105 transactions spiked at quarter-ends, Lehman's ordinary repo balances dropped off significantly during the same time periods.

Illustration 5: Repo 105 Plus Paying Down Liabilities

In the Repo 105 transaction, Lehman would use the cash it generated to reduce traditional borrowings, such as ordinary repos ("Collateralized financings" in the table below). By applying the cash from a Repo 105 transaction to pay down liabilities created by ordinary repos, Lehman reduced its balance sheet and leverage.

Assets (in millions)		Liabilities	
Cash	$ 7,500	Short-term borrowings	$ 200,000
Financial instruments	**300,000**	Collateralized financings	**275,000**
Collateralized agreements	350,000	Long-term borrowings	150,000
Receivables	20,000	Payables	98,000
Other	72,500	Stockholders' equity	27,000
Total	**$ 750,000**		**$ 750,000**

When the Repo 105 transaction matured, Lehman borrowed funds to repay the Repo 105 cash borrowing plus interest, and the previously transferred securities inventory returned to Lehman's balance sheet as securities inventory. Accordingly, total assets and total liabilities increased.

Although it is undisputed that Lehman received cash as part of Repo 105 transactions, the documents reveal that the financing Lehman received under Repo 105 transactions was not the real or primary purpose for entering into these transactions. Lehman could have obtained the same financing at a lower cost by engaging in ordinary repo transactions with substantially the same counterparties and using the same assets involved in the Repo 105 transactions.

Requirement A:

1. What is a repurchase agreement? What is a sale and repurchase agreement?
2. What is leverage? What is the gross leverage and net leverage for Illustrations 4 and 5? Why is leverage significant for a firm?
3. Identify Lehman's primary motive for undertaking tens of billions of dollars in Repo 105 transactions at or near each quarter-end in late 20X1 and 20X2.
4. Are Illustrations 4 and 5 proper under U.S. GAAP? If not, what GAAP rule or principle do they violate?

B. Repo 105 Practice

Starting in mid-20X1, the market began demanding that investment banks reduce their leverage, a crisis of major proportions for Lehman. The inability to reduce leverage could lead to a ratings downgrade, which would have had an immediate, tangible monetary impact on Lehman. The senior vice president for external reporting wrote that the "question" of net leverage ratio "has come up multiple times in the 20 seconds that I've been here—largely from CFOs, Corporate Strategy, Investor Relations and the like."

By January 20X2, Lehman's CEO Fuld ordered a firmwide deleveraging strategy, hoping to reduce the firm's positions in commercial and residential real estate and leveraged loans in particular by half. In the words of one internal Lehman presentation, "Reducing leverage is necessary to remove refinancing risk and win back the confidence of the market, lenders, and investors."

Lehman believed that "net leverage based on net assets and tangible equity capital" was "a more meaningful measure of leverage" than gross leverage. In its Forms 10-K and 10-Q, Lehman defined its "net leverage ratio" as net assets divided by tangible equity capital. Lehman defined net assets as total assets, excluding (1) cash and securities segregated and on deposit for regulatory and other purposes, (2) securities received as collateral, (3) securities purchases under agreements to resell, (4) securities borrowed, and (5) identifiable intangible assets and goodwill. Lehman calculated tangible equity capital by including stockholders' equity and junior subordinated notes and excluding identifiable intangible assets and goodwill. In contrast, Lehman's "leverage ratio" was generally computed by simply dividing total assets by stockholders' equity.

From 20X0, when Lehman first began using Repo 105 transactions, until early to mid-20X1, Lehman engaged in a relatively consistent volume of Repo 105 transactions, including at quarter-end, generally within a range of between $20 and $25 billion. Lehman also maintained internal rules—based on senior management's judgment rather than any accounting requirement—limiting the total firmwide use of Repo 105 transactions to $25 billion.

Lehman regularly increased its use of Repo 105 transactions in the days prior to reporting periods in order to reduce its publicly reported net leverage and liabilities on its balance sheet. Although Lehman had, in effect, borrowed tens of billions of dollars in these transactions, Lehman's periodic reports did not disclose the cash "borrowings" and the known obligation to repay the debt. Lehman used the cash from the Repo 105 transactions to pay down other liabilities, thereby reducing both the total liabilities and the total assets reported on its balance sheet and lowering its leverage ratios. A few days after the new quarter began, Lehman would borrow the necessary funds to repay the cash borrowing plus interest, repurchase the securities, and restore the assets to its balance sheet.

Lehman never publicly disclosed its use of Repo 105 transactions, its accounting treatment for these transactions, the considerable escalation of its total Repo 105 usage in late 20X1 and into 20X2, or the material impact these transactions had on the firm's publicly reported net leverage ratio.

According to former Global Financial Controller Martin Kelly, a careful review of Lehman's Forms 10-K and 10-Q would not reveal Lehman's use of Repo 105 transactions. Lehman failed to disclose its Repo 105 practice even though Kelly believed "that the only purpose or motive for the transactions was reduction in the balance sheet." He also felt that "there was no substance to the transactions" and expressed concerns with Lehman's Repo 105 program to two consecutive Lehman CFOs. He advised them that the lack of economic substance to Repo 105 transactions meant "reputational risk" to Lehman if the firm's use of the transactions became known to the public. In addition to its material omissions, Lehman affirmatively misrepresented in its financial statements that the firm treated all repo transactions as financing transactions for financial reporting purposes.

In light of these factors, Lehman relied at an increasing pace on Repo 105 transactions at each quarter-end in late 20X1 and early 20X2. Lehman's expansion of its Repo 105 program mitigated, in part, the adverse impact its increasingly "sticky"/illiquid inventory—made up mostly of the leveraged loans and residential and commercial real estate positions CEO Fuld wanted to exit—was having on the firm's publicly reported net leverage and net balance sheet.

An early 20X1 document from Lehman's archives concluded that "Repo 105 offers a low cost way to offset the balance sheet and leverage impact of current market conditions" and further stated that "[e]xiting large CMBS positions in Real Estate and sub-prime loans in Mortgages before quarter end would incur large losses due to the steep discounts that they would have to be offered at and carry substantial reputation risk in the market. . . . A Repo 105 increase would help avoid this without negatively impacting our leverage ratios." While Lehman did not utilize Repo 105 transactions for selling sticky inventory, the firm's expanded use of Repo 105 transactions at quarter-end impacted Lehman's publicly reported net leverage ratio.

In this way, unknown to the investing public, rating agencies, government regulators, and Lehman's Board of Directors, Lehman reverse engineered the firm's net leverage ratio for public consumption. Notably, during Lehman's 20X2 earnings calls in which it touted its leverage reduction, analysts frequently inquired about *the means* by which Lehman was reducing its leverage. The CFO told analysts that Lehman was "trying to give the group a great amount of transparency on the balance sheet." Yet she reported that Lehman was reducing its leverage through the sale of less liquid asset categories. She said nothing about the firm's use of Repo 105 transactions.

Lehman was unable to find a U.S. law firm that would provide it with an opinion letter permitting the true sale accounting treatment. Lehman resorted to an opinion letter by the prestigious Linklaters law firm in London and began to conduct its Repo 105 program under the shield of the letter. The law firm wrote the opinion letter for Lehman's European broker-dealer in London, under English law. Accordingly, if U.S.-based Lehman entities wished to engage in a Repo 105 transaction, they transferred their securities inventory to the subsidiary in England in order to conduct the transaction on their behalf.

Beginning in mid-20X1—the very time that the market began to particularly focus on investment banks' leverage—Lehman breached its internal limit on Repo 105 activity at every quarter-end, temporarily removing as much as $50.4 billion in securities inventory from its balance sheet in the second quarter of 20X2.

Lehman dramatically ramped up its use of Repo 105 transactions in late 20X1 and early 20X2 despite concerns about the practice expressed by Lehman officers and personnel. In an April 20X2 email asking if he was familiar with the use of Repo 105 transactions to reduce the net balance sheet, Bart McDade, Lehman's former head of equities (20X0–20X2) and president and chief operating officer (COO) (June–September 20X2), replied: "I am very aware . . . it is another drug we are on." A week earlier McDade had recommended to Lehman's Executive Committee that the firm set a cap on the use of Repo 105 transactions.

A senior member of Lehman's Finance Group considered Lehman's Repo 105 program to be balance sheet "window-dressing" that was "based on legal technicalities." Other former Lehman employees characterized Repo 105 transactions as an "accounting gimmick" and a "lazy way of managing the balance sheet."

The head of the Liquid Markets Group within the division wrote at the same quarter-end regarding the group's balance sheet: "We have a desperate situation and I need another 2 billion from you, either through Repo 105 or outright sales. Cost is irrelevant, we need to do it." Lehman's reliance on Repo 105 transactions for quarter-end balance sheet relief continued into Lehman's second quarter of 20X2. In an email titled "Q2 balance sheet" and dated May 21, 20X2—ten days before Lehman's second-quarter close—the head of the Liquid Markets Group wrote: "Do as much as you can in Repo 105" in response to the question "Do u think we can be flexible beyond $3bn in 105?" In another May 21, 20X2, email, the head of Liquid Markets asked: "Are we going to make the European balance sheet target," which elicited the response: "V close . . . anything that moves is getting 105'd."

Lehman had the ability to conduct an ordinary repo transaction using the same securities and with substantially the same counterparties as in the Repo 105 transactions, and at a lower cost. As such, several former Lehman personnel uniformly acknowledged that the overarching goal of Repo 105 transactions was to meet net balance sheet targets. Thus, the goal was to reduce the net asset component (the numerator) of the net leverage ratio calculation in connection with the filing of Lehman's financial statements.

Audit walk-through papers prepared by Lehman's outside auditor, Ernst & Young, regarding the process for reopening or adjusting a closed balance sheet stated: "Materiality is usually defined as any item individually, or in the aggregate, that moves net leverage by 0.1 or more (typically $1.8 billion)." Repo 105 moved net leverage not by tenths, but by whole points.

Lehman's publicly reported net leverage ratios for the fourth quarter of 20X1, the first quarter of 20X2, and the second quarter of 20X2 were 16.1x, 15.4x, and 12.1x, respectively. Without the balance sheet benefit of Repo 105 transactions, Lehman's net leverage ratios for the same periods would have been 17.8x, 17.3x, and 13.9x, respectively. Lehman's directors, the rating agencies, and government regulators—all of whom were unaware of Lehman's use of Repo 105 transactions—have commented that Lehman's Repo 105 usage was material or significant information that they would have wanted to know.

Requirement B: Repo Accounting

5. In your own words, describe repo accounting, and identify some of the difficulties that arise in the handling of these types of transactions.

6. We often hear the phrase "substance over form" in accounting. Define "substance over form," and explain how this concept applies in the Lehman case.

7. What is the accounting justification for Lehman treating the Repo 105 transactions as sales as opposed to financing transactions? In other words, what loophole was Lehman trying to wiggle through by collateralizing the transaction with 105% (hence the Repo 105 label) of the amount advanced?

8. Accounting for transfers and servicing of financial assets was specifically addressed by Financial Accounting Standard No. 140. One element that is addressed in this standard regarding the treatment as a "sale" or refinance is the concept of control. How does the ASC explain when the transferor has surrendered control over transferred assets?

9. Identify Lehman's primary motive for undertaking tens of billions of dollars in Repo 105 transactions at or near each quarter-end in late 20X1 and 20X2.

10. What subsequently happened to Lehman Brothers?

Readings

Michael Corkery and Susanne Craig, "Lehman's Bet on a California Developer Yields a Lesson on Downside of a Boom," *Wall Street Journal*, September 3, 2008, Eastern edition, C.1.

Michael J. De La Merced and Julia Werdigier, "The Origins of Lehman's 'Repo 105' New York Times Dealbook," March 12, 2010. http://dealbook.nytimes.com/2010/03/12/the-british-origins-of-lehmans-accounting-gimmick/.

Jeffrey McCracken, "Lehman's Chaotic Bankruptcy Filing Destroyed Billions in Value," *Wall Street Journal*, December 29, 2008, Eastern edition, A.10.

Linda Sandler, "$1 Billion to Clean Up Lehman," *Business Week*, August 2, 2010, Eastern edition, 1.

Franziska Scheven, "Lehman's Failure: 'Rotten at the Head'," *Institutional Investor*, October, 2010,

Sources: Anton R. Valukas, Examiner's Report on Lehman Brothers Holding Inc., 2010. lehmanreport.jenner.com. Lehman Brothers Holding Inc. (LBHI) 2007 Form 10-K, on p. 97.

Case 9

Nortel: Revenue Recognition

Substantial excerpts from Nortel Networks Corporation's (Nortel's) public record are used for this case. Nortel is a Canadian corporation whose business consists of design, development, assembly, marketing, sale, licensing, installation, servicing, and support for networking solutions. Nortel's common stock trades publicly on the New York and Toronto Stock Exchanges under the symbol NT.

For many years, Nortel's corporate culture was shaped by its attitude toward targets and goals. It was understood across the company that either missing or exceeding a financial target reflected a failure to manage the company's business properly. Frank Dunn, acting as CFO and later as president and CEO, continually reinforced this culture by, among other things, reviewing and inquiring about particular accounting entries during the quarterly and year-end closing processes. Dunn had a well-known disregard for internal accounting and financial controls. In that environment, the accounting system did not act as a control system and, moreover, did not necessarily measure

Nortel's performance. Instead, Nortel's executives and finance managers treated their accounting records as mere tools to meet the company's financial objectives.

In January 20X1, Nortel began reporting its results under U.S. GAAP. In the meantime, the company did not update its internal accounting guidelines to conform to U.S. GAAP and offered only sporadic and superficial training to its employees. In this regard, Nortel created an environment that would selectively apply or disregard U.S. GAAP concepts as desired to meet its financial targets.

A. Revenue Recognition Practices

On July 25, 20X1, Nortel made public its financial results for the second quarter of 20X1 (Second Quarter 20X1 Earnings Release) and also announced that it was raising its outlook for the remainder of 20X1. The company's revised outlook primed the market to expect 40% revenue growth from Nortel for the year, up from Nortel's previous guidance of 30%. Nortel also indicated that investors should expect operating earnings growth in the "high 30s." During an earnings conference with analysts on the same day (Second Quarter 20X1 Earnings Call), analysts were told that Nortel's second-quarter results and its newly announced expectation for the year were attributable to the performance of its optical business:

> [The growth] is being driven obviously by a very, very strong performance of our optical business. Revenue growth in optical in [the second] quarter was, once again, 150%. I think the last time that we had this call we talked about our ambitions to break $10 billion of shipments in optical business this year. Now we feel quite comfortable we'll exceed that number and we'll have a number for the year that will be somewhere north of $10 billion of shipment for the year.

Nortel's CEO at that time later suggested that optical revenues might possibly reach $12 billion. The Second Quarter 20X1 Earnings Release also attributed Nortel's revised growth expectations to "the momentum we have been experiencing during the first half of this year, supported by an 85 percent increase in order input and a 1.35 book to bill in the quarter." With respect to the third quarter of 20X1, Nortel told analysts: "We are gaining momentum so we do have a very solid quarter coming."

Third Quarter 20X1: Nortel Withholds Its Plummeting Internal Expectations

Soon after releasing its second quarter 20X1 financials, Nortel experienced an extreme softening of orders. This softening of orders caused Nortel to lower its internal expectations for the rest of the year. During the month of September 20X1, internal forecasts for Nortel's business units showed that the company expected to miss its third-quarter revenue targets by at least $405 million and its third-quarter earnings targets by at least $506 million.

By October 17, 20X1, Nortel determined that its yearly revenues were off from expectations by more than $1 billion from expectations. Nortel's business unit finance personnel noted: "Lost $1.9 [billion in] 2nd half [20X1] revenue over last 4 weeks"; "Margin shows no sign of recovery"; and "1st half 20X2 already $1.5 [billion] off expectation."

Anticipated orders from multiple large customers were, in some cases, below expectations by hundreds of millions of dollars. The optical sales forecast was at least $500 million below the $10 billion to $12 billion level for which Nortel had primed the market. At the time, it was also noted that third quarter 20X1 revenues were $900 million less than Nortel originally had budgeted. Further, as of October 17, 20X1, Nortel's expected fourth quarter 20X1 earnings were at least $320 million short of the amount needed to meet consensus earnings per share.

Although this information was quite unsettling for Nortel and its management, the company did not share any of this information with the public. Instead, it continued to make optimistic forecasts that could not be met through operations alone. Nortel made public its earnings release for the third quarter on October 24, 20X1, reporting third-quarter revenues of $7.3 billion and net earnings of $575 million (or 18 cents per share). Even though its earnings for the quarter exceeded analyst expectations by 1 cent per share, analysts expressed concern that revenues came in at the low end of the expected range of $7.3 billion to $7.8 billion.

During Nortel's third quarter 20X1 earnings call, analysts expressed concern about Nortel's sales of optical Internet gear and questioned whether Nortel expected lower optical sales for the remainder of 20X1. The company reassured analysts that it expected to sell out of its optical gear in the fourth quarter and rejected the suggestion that there was a slowdown in performance or growth. Instead, it blamed third-quarter results primarily on (1) slow installations of optical equipment and (2) customers who were working through existing supplies, but were expected to place orders in the fourth quarter of 20X1.

Nortel told the public there was no change in its guidance for 20X1 and reaffirmed its prior-announced growth expectations for 20X1, stating: "We continue to expect that our percentage growth in revenue and earnings per share from operations in 20X1 . . . will be in the low 40's." Nortel continued to predict that "annual optical equipment sales will surpass $10 billion" in 20X1; however, there was no mention of the $12 billion optical sales figure that Nortel's then CEO had mentioned as a possibility in September 20X1. As a consequence, Nortel's stock price fell more than 34% over the next two days.

In light of the circumstances, external pressure to increase revenues mounted. Particular pressure focused on the sales of optical equipment, which, at the time, made up a significant portion of Nortel's revenues and were closely followed by analysts. In an attempt to alleviate this pressure, Nortel, led by the CFO and controller, embarked on a scheme to manipulate its results for the remainder of 20X1 through accounting changes.

Fourth Quarter 20X1: Nortel Manipulates Its Revenue Recognition Policies

In late October 20X1, the controller met with other senior finance managers to discuss ways to increase the company's revenues. Central to the discussion was Nortel's revenue recognition policies and their effect on Nortel's ability to reach its revenue targets for 20X1.

The company was particularly eager to find a solution for the hundreds of millions of dollars in inventory (consisting primarily of optical products) sitting in its warehouses and offsite storage locations. As U.S. GAAP generally requires goods to be delivered first to the buyer, revenues could not be recognized for this inventory.

The increase in inventory at Nortel was driven by both external and internal factors. For example, Nortel's inventory levels had grown, in part, because orders for its optical inventory had slowed and because the company had experienced some delays in optical installation. Additionally, internal decisions by Nortel required the banning of bill and hold transactions from the company's sales and accounting practices. A bill and hold transaction is one where the customer agrees to purchase a product, but the seller (here Nortel) retains physical possession until the customer can accept delivery. Once revenues are recognized, the product no longer appears on the seller's books as inventory. Nortel could no longer recognize as revenue, or remove from inventory, equipment that had been sold, but not yet delivered.

Nortel banned bill and hold transactions because its executives concluded that U.S. GAAP requirements for such transactions were too difficult to meet. Also, such transactions were being "scrutinized" by the SEC, and the second quarter 20X1 revenues were sufficiently robust without the use of such transactions. However, throughout the third and fourth quarters of 20X1, as revenue pressures and inventory levels increased, and as Wall Street increasingly focused on Nortel's optical numbers, areas of possible manipulation were identified, and pressure mounted for Nortel to repeal the ban. Nortel's ban on bill and hold transactions was short-lived.

Reintroduction of Bill and Hold Transactions

In late October 20X1, as a first step toward reintroducing bill and hold transactions into Nortel's sales and accounting practices, Nortel's then controller and assistant controller asked Nortel's outside auditor to answer the following: (1) "Under what circumstances can revenue be recognized on product (merchandise) that has not been shipped to the end customer?" (2) Can merchandise accounting be used to recognize revenues "when installation is imminent" or "when installation is considered to be a minor portion of the contract"?

On November 2, 20X1, the outside auditors presented Nortel with a set of charts that explained U.S. GAAP criteria for revenues to be recognized prior to delivery (including additional factors to consider for a bill and hold transaction) as well as providing an example of a customer request for a bill and hold sale "that would support the assertion that Nortel should recognize revenue" prior to delivery.

On November 7, 20X1, Nortel internally distributed its own revenue recognition guidance, which consisted of charts that had been drafted by Nortel's controller. Nortel's guidance announced a change in accounting policy for sales of various products, including optical products, which previously had been accounted for under a percentage of completion method. Now the sale of these products could be recorded using merchandise accounting and be sold using bill and hold transactions.

Nortel's guidance provided to its staff omitted some key portions of the outside auditor's presentation relating to U.S. GAAP requirements for bill and hold transactions. The outside auditor had reviewed Nortel's guidance before November 7, 20X1, and warned Nortel that it was too brief and did not give the intended users—Nortel's accounting and finance personnel—sufficient information to always make the correct assessment of the appropriate accounting treatment. The outside auditor requested that Nortel distribute the outside auditor's guidance as well, but Nortel declined.

On November 8, 20X1, Nortel's controller informed the recipients of Nortel's revenue recognition guidance—certain Nortel accounting and finance employees—that Nortel was having difficulty meeting its fourth quarter 20X1 revenue targets and that bill and hold transactions were being reintroduced to assist Nortel in meeting those targets. He directed them to formulate a plan to implement the new guidance.

A plan was developed within days to approach and urge customers unlikely to take delivery of ordered inventory by year-end to execute "risk of loss letters" (Nortel's parlance for bill and hold transactions). In an effort to create the false appearance that the Nortel-initiated risk of loss letters had been customer-initiated, Nortel typically submitted the letter to the customer to be printed on customer letterhead. Nortel's controller and assistant controller understood that the proposed plan would lead to transactions not consistent with U.S. GAAP, or the outside auditor's guidance, but with the knowledge and acquiescence or recklessness of Nortel's CFO, they approved the plan anyway.

In order to implement the new bill and hold accounting strategy, Nortel systematically approached the following customers in 20X1: (1) customers that previously had placed orders, (2) customers that told Nortel they expected to place orders and take delivery in 20X2, and (3) new customers. Nortel induced such customers with offers of price discounts, interest deferments, and extended billing terms. Although many transactions were completed during this time period, the vast majority of transactions entered into had no substantial business purpose for the buyer.

As part of its restatement, Nortel reversed approximately $1 billion in revenues that had been improperly recognized in the fourth quarter of 20X1 through these bill and hold transactions.

Requirement A: Bill and Hold

1. When does U.S. GAAP permit revenue from a bill and hold transaction to be recognized?
2. How does IFRS compare with U.S. GAAP on bill and hold transactions?
3. Answer Nortel's questions: (1) "Under what circumstances can revenue be recognized on product (merchandise) that has not been shipped to the end customer?" (2) Can merchandise accounting be used to recognize revenues "when installation is imminent" or "when installation is considered to be a minor portion of the contract"?
4. If you were the controller of Nortel, how could you have prevented the problem from arising?

B. Recognition of Revenues on Sales to a Pass-Through Entity

In the fourth quarter of 20X1, Nortel recognized revenues upon delivery of millions of dollars of its goods to Telamon Corporation (Telamon), a pass-through entity for certain business deals.

Nortel used Telamon, a minority-owned business, to satisfy the business requirements of Nortel customers who were required to make a percentage of purchases from minority- or women-owned businesses. Accordingly, rather than purchasing Nortel's products directly, they purchased Nortel's products from Telamon.

Even though Telamon did not accept the risks of ownership, Nortel recognized revenue when it delivered the goods. Telamon could not (and did not) pay for the products until such products had been resold and Telamon had received payment from the end customer. Telamon also routinely returned unsold products to Nortel. Indeed, in 20X1, Telamon returned hundreds of millions of dollars of goods to Nortel that it was unable to resell due to softening orders.

In the fourth quarter of 20X1, Nortel's controller considered, but ultimately rejected, the idea of changing its practice to recognize revenues on Telamon sales only when the end customer had paid for the goods. Nortel's CFO, controller, and assistant controller likewise discussed revenue recognition, but decided against correcting the policy during the 20X1 year-end closing processes. In both instances, the decisions were influenced by the fact that changing the practice would negatively impact Nortel's revenues for its optical business unit. Nortel recognized approximately $150 million in revenues for sales to Telamon in the fourth quarter of 20X1.

Recognition of Revenues before Passage of Title

As part of the fourth quarter 20X1 push to increase revenues, Nortel also recognized revenues on certain sales at the time of product shipment even though title to the product did not pass until delivery had been made to the customer. The company conveniently assumed that delivery typically occurred within seven days of shipment. No testing was done to validate the assumption, and it was ultimately incorrect.

Recognition of Revenues for Substituted Products

Another push-for-revenue scheme resulted in Nortel recognizing revenues during 20X1 for an optical upgrade product known as DX3 that was not yet available for shipment. Specifically, in the fourth quarter of 20X1, as a result of product delays, Nortel was unable to deliver the DX3 product. It implemented a temporary work-around to deliver the capacity of the DX3 upgrade by shipping two DX1 products—which had the combined capacity of one DX3—to serve as a placeholder until the DX3 could be completed. Nortel recognized revenues as if it had delivered the DX3 product. This manipulation in revenues contributed to Nortel's ability to meet its public guidance of $10 billion in optical revenues for fourth quarter of 20X1.

Nortel's Fourth Quarter 20X1 Earnings Release and 20X1 Form 10-K

On January 18, 20X2, Nortel issued an earnings release that made public its financial results for the fourth quarter of 20X1 (Fourth Quarter 20X1 Earnings Release). The release reported revenues of $8.8 billion for the fourth quarter (a 34% increase from the corresponding quarter in 20X0) and revenues of $30.3 billion for the year (a 42% increase from 20X0). The release stated that "the fourth quarter capped a year of exceptional growth, which was in line with . . . expectations." Included in the release was tremendous praise for Nortel's optical revenues, which "topped $10 billion for the year, more than doubling 20X0 revenues" and which were attributed to "strong growth" in the United States and other geographic regions. Although these results represented a lower growth rate than in prior years, Nortel confidently confirmed its financial guidance for fiscal year 20X2, saying that it expected revenue and earnings to grow by 30% in 20X2.

When to issue the Fourth Quarter 20X1 Earnings Release was very strategically considered. Nortel carefully crafted the timing of its Fourth Quarter 20X1 Earnings Release to mislead investors about its performance just long enough for it to complete a $2.5 billion acquisition in February 20X2. On February 13, 20X2, with the benefit of an artificially inflated share price, Nortel paid $2.5 billion to acquire a competitor's Swiss subsidiary and related assets in New York.

On March 31, 20X2, Nortel filed with the SEC its annual report on Form 10-K for the period ending December 31, 20X1. The 20X1 Form 10-K reported revenues of $8.8 billion for the fourth quarter of 20X1 and $30.3 billion for the year. The Form 10-K also represented that the financial statements therein were prepared in conformity with U.S. GAAP.

Requirement B:

5. When does U.S. GAAP recognize revenue from sales to a pass-through entity?
6. How does IFRS compare with U.S. GAAP on this issue?
7. Summarize how Nortel justified recognizing its revenue on sales to a pass-through entity.
8. Were Nortel's revenue recognition manipulations successful?
9. What strategic decisions were made in this case?
10. When does the culture of a company change its accounting practices?

Readings

Marco Aiolfi, Marius Rodriguez, and Allan Timmermann, "Understanding Analysts' Earnings Expectations: Biases, Nonlinearities, and Predictability," *Journal of Financial Econometrics* 8, no. 3 (Summer 2010): 305.

Ken Brown and Mark Heinzl, "Reversing the Charges: Nortel Board Finds Accounting Tricks behind '03 Profits; A Telecom Star Manipulated Its Reserves, Hid Losses, An Investigation Discovers; How to Empty the Cookie Jar," *Wall Street Journal*, July 2, 2004, Eastern edition, A.1.

Gin Chong, "Is Income Smoothing Ethical?" *The Journal of Corporate Accounting and Finance* 18, no. 1 (November–December 2006): 41.

Jennifer Francis, Dhananjay Nanda, and Per Olsson, "Voluntary Disclosure, Earnings Quality, and Cost of Capital," *Journal of Accounting Research* 46, no. 1 (March 2008): 53.

Mark W. Nelson, John A. Elliott, and Robin L. Tarpley, "How Are Earnings Managed? Examples from Auditors," *Accounting Horizons* 17 (2003): 17.

Sources: SEC, Accounting and Auditing Enforcement Release No. 2818, April 30, 2008.
SEC, Accounting and Auditing Enforcement Release No. 2740, October 15, 2007.
SEC, Accounting and Auditing Enforcement Release No. 2676, September 12, 2007.
SEC, Accounting and Auditing Enforcement Release No. 2576, March 12, 2007.
SEC, Staff Accounting Bulletin No. 101, December 3, 1999.
Securities and Exchange Commission v. Nortel Networks Corporation, Civil Action No. 07-CV-8851 (S.D.N.Y.) (This case uses substantial excerpts from this public record).

Case 10

Sycamore Networks

A. Backdated Stock Options

This case uses substantial excerpts from the opinion by Vice Chancellor Strine of the Delaware Chancery Court and a related SEC Accounting and Auditing Enforcement Release as the basis for its simplified version of the events and predicament that Sycamore Networks, Inc. (Sycamore), faced.

Sycamore developed and marketed optical networking products. Since going public, Sycamore's share price had fluctuated widely. The initial public offering in January 20X0 was at $38 per share. From there, the stock went up to a high of more than $165 per share in August 20X0. By 20X1, its shares were trading below $10 and currently trade between $3 and $4.

Stock options were a particularly important component of Sycamore's employee recruitment and retention compensation packages because the company paid below-average salaries. In 20X7, the SEC and the U.S. Department of Justice launched investigations into Sycamore's stock options practices based on the suspicion that Sycamore had misrepresented—by backdating—certain options grants and had engaged in related misbehavior such as "bullet dodging." Bullet-dodging options are granted just after the company releases negative information to the market, thereby allowing the recipient the benefit of a lower exercise price that reflects the price decline caused by the negative information.

The 20X1 grants were made with an exercise price of $4 per share. Ten days earlier, Sycamore's shares were trading at $5 apiece. Twenty days after the grants, the shares were back up to $6. The 20X3 grants were made at an exercise price of $5 per share. Twenty days after the grants, the stock price was above $7.

The plaintiff, John S. Desimone, filed a complaint in Delaware Chancery Court. Desimone challenged two different types of options grants. The first category involves grants of options to Sycamore's rank-and-file employees and to its officers (the Incentive Plan). The second category involves grants of options to Sycamore's outside directors (the Outside Director Plan). Each of the four nonemployee Sycamore directors received his pro rata share of these options.

The Sycamore stockholders approved the issuance of the exact number of options to be awarded annually to the outside directors and the date of issuance. Desimone alleged that in two of the years, the plan-specified date of issuance was preceded by the regular disclosure of an earnings release containing negative information. The Outside Director Plan automatically granted 30,000 options to each of Sycamore's outside directors each year on the date of Sycamore's annual stockholders meeting. The Outside Director Plan also required that the exercise price of those options be equal to 100% of the fair market value of Sycamore's stock on the date of the grant. The options granted under the Outside Director Plan were subject to a three-year vesting schedule that prevented the recipients from realizing any immediate value from the options. Under the schedule, a third of the options vested after one year, another third after two years, and the last third three years from the date of the grant.

The Incentive Plan (providing for officer and employee grants) stated that "[t]he Incentive Plan will be administered by a committee appointed by the Board of Directors of the Company . . . and consisting of two or more members of the Board." Importantly, it also provides that the board may delegate to one or more executive officers of the company the power to grant stock rights and exercise such other powers under the plan as the board may determine. However, the Board shall fix the maximum number of shares subject to stock rights, and such executive officers shall set the maximum number of shares for any one participant. In other words, with few limitations, the Incentive Plan contemplated that Sycamore's directors themselves might have a very limited role in making certain options grants by permitting the board to delegate its authority under the plan to Sycamore's executive officers.

Importantly, the Incentive Plan differs from the Outside Director Plan in that it does not require that all options grants be priced at fair market value on the date of the grant. Rather, the Incentive Plan merely states that the exercise price per share will be set at the discretion of those charged with administering the plan. To be clear that the Incentive Plan contemplated issuance of non-fair-market-value options, the options pricing section of the plan contained a carve-out requiring only that options intended to qualify as incentive stock options under § 422(b) of the Internal Revenue Code be priced at no less than 100% of fair market value on the option grant date. Section 422(b) permits the recipient of a qualifying option grant to recognize no income as a result of the grant if the corporation does not take a deduction attributable to it.

Jewels, formerly a CPA, was well versed in the relevant stock option accounting principles. During her entire tenure as Sycamore's CFO, Jewels was the primary person responsible for the preparation of the financial statements included in Sycamore's public filings. She also ensured that stock compensation expenses were properly reported. Kalinen, the COO, also was aware of the relevant accounting principles related to stock options. Jewels and Kalinen knew that Sycamore was required to record in its books and records, and report in its financial statements, compensation expenses related to "in the money" options. Jewels and Kalinen knew that Sycamore did not report appropriate compensation expenses related to the officer grants in its financial statements included in its public filings with the SEC. Nearly $4 million in compensation expenses related to these stock option grants.

One example of improper stock options backdating at Sycamore occurred in connection with the company's "refresh" grants. Through its refresh program, the company periodically granted options to large numbers of existing employees as an incentive for them to remain with the company. In some cases, the options were granted to supplement options that were "underwater" because the market price of Sycamore's stock had fallen below the exercise price of the options.

Specifically, in an effort to create the impression that certain employees had started working at Sycamore on dates that they had not, Friedman altered or created, or caused others to alter or create, company payroll or personnel records, such as job offer letters and records in the human resources database, that reflected inaccurate start dates for certain employees.

Sycamore's options practices became controversial when Sycamore's former director of human resources, Stephen Landry, publicly accused Sycamore of backdating options. Sycamore hired Landry in the winter of 20X0 and allegedly "eased him out" of the company in the fall of 20X0. Upon his exit, Landry entered into a severance agreement with Sycamore, which he negotiated with defendant Jewels, Sycamore's then CFO. That severance agreement granted Landry a number of stock options. When Sycamore's stock price declined sharply in the following years, those options went underwater, and Landry's severance package became worthless.

An internal memo (Memo) separately discussed each employee's options and suggested various courses of action designed to cover up the fact that the grant dates were being manipulated. Substantial covert actions were detailed to avoid having the backdating operation detected, and the Memo made a "risk assessment" for the actions taken with respect to each employee. The Memo considered many of the cover-up actions to be "low risk." For example, for one of the employees, the Memo stated, "She is a rank and file employee and the Company has no prior experience with her (although she does have a relationship with [another Sycamore employee] that could work to our advantage should the risk of exposure on this agreement surface). Low audit risk (exposure on payroll registers and on the medical insurance effective dates, both of which will remain unchanged[;] however, the auditors never reference these documents in their audits)."

For others, the risk was higher: "There is an audit risk since the [stock option] grant was originally issued in the first quarter (Q1) and the cancellation occurred after the Q1 audit." Another example concerned a newly hired employee in Sycamore's legal department whose option grant date was manipulated. The Memo stated: "Requires new offer letter for the file to adjust the salary difference from her actual date of hire 11/27/X0 and 12/21/X0. Adjustment will be addressed in the offer letter in the form of a sign on bonus."

Upon learning of the Memo, Sycamore's audit committee launched an investigation into Sycamore's historic accounting for stock option grants.

Requirement A:

1. What are the current accounting requirements under U.S. GAAP for stock options? Give the authority.
2. What are the types of stock options, and how do the types differ in accounting treatment?
3. Did Sycamore violate GAAP? If so, how?

B. Spring-Loaded Options

Even more so than backdating, the "spring loading" of stock options presents doctrinally complex issues. The practice involves making market-value options grants at a time when the company possesses, but has not yet released, favorable, material, nonpublic information that will likely increase the stock price when disclosed.

Consider this example: A corporation has been engaged in serious efforts to land a so-called merger of equals. The CFO and COO have missed their summer vacations, their children's baseball games, and every important family occasion for four months while working on the transaction. The CEO recommends to the independent compensation committee that it make special awards of options as bonuses to the CFO and COO for their extraordinary efforts. The committee agrees that this is warranted and makes the awards in advance of the announcement of the merger agreement, recognizing that the announcement will likely increase the company's stock price. The corporation's stock option plan does not require that all options be issued at fair market value on the date of grant.

In the merger proxy for this example, it is clearly disclosed that the CFO and COO received the grants in recognition of their efforts in connection with securing the merger. Assume that the options will vest and be exercisable if the merger is consummated and that the corporation has accounted for the options as fair-market-value awards. The corporation in good faith relies on the advice of tax and accounting advisors, which is expected to be consistent with applicable regulatory law, especially given that the merger was subject to several closing conditions. In this context, there is no deception with respect to the corporation's stockholders, as the directors have fully disclosed why they made the award. All of these factors—the candor of the directors about the reason for the grant, their compliance with the terms of the relevant plan, and their good-faith reliance on experts—are of great relevance to a court considering the appropriateness of the options. The fundamental issue is whether the directors have made a rational compensation decision.

Requirement B: Stock Options

4. As compared to backdated options, do spring-loaded options violate U.S. GAAP? Give the authority.
5. Compare and contrast backdated, spring-loaded, and bullet-dodging stock options.
6. Do you agree or disagree with the board of directors' decision to grant stock options as described in the hypothetical case? Why?
7. Should a company issue stock options to directors, executives, and employees? Explain.
8. What precautions should a company that issues stock options take with regard to those stock options?

Readings

Tim V. Eaton and Ryan J. Patterson, "Underwater Stock Compensation," *The CPA Journal* 80, no. 11 (November 2010): 58.

Theo Francis, "Another Consequence of Backdated Options: Stiff Tax Bills," *Wall Street Journal*, December 12, 2006, Eastern edition, B.1.

Pete H. Oppenheimer, "Legal and Accounting Issues of Manipulating the Timing of Stock Option Grants," *Journal of Financial Crime* 18, no. 1 (2011): 63.

Sue Ravenscroft and Paul F. Williams, "Making Imaginary Worlds Real: The Case of Expensing Employee Stock Options," *Accounting, Organizations and Society* 34, no. 6/7 (October 2009): 770.

David A. Reppenhagen, "Contagion of Accounting Methods: Evidence from Stock Option Expensing," *Review of Accounting Studies* 15, no. 3 (September 2010): 629.

Sources: *John S. Desimone v. Sycamore Networks, Inc.*, 924 A.2d 908 (Del. Ch. 2007).
SEC, Accounting and Auditing Enforcement Release No. 2848, July 28, 2008.
SEC, Accounting and Auditing Enforcement Release No. 2843, July 9, 2008.
SEC v. Sycamore Networks, Inc., Civil Action No. 1:08-CV-11166 (DPW) (D. Mass. July 2008).

INDEX